PRACTICE MAKES PERFECT

Mastering Writing

PRACTICE MAKES PERFECT

Mastering Writing

Gary Robert Muschla

New York   Chicago   San Francisco   Lisbon   London   Madrid   Mexico City
Milan   New Delhi   San Juan   Seoul   Singapore   Sydney   Toronto

A version of this book was previously published under the title *Teach Terrific Writing,
Grades 6–8*.

16 17 18 19 20 LBC 28 27 26 25 24

ISBN 978-0-07-174716-5
MHID   0-07-174716-8

Library of Congress Control Number: 2010926964

McGraw-Hill books are available at special quantity discounts to use as premiums and
sales promotions or for use in corporate training programs. To contact a representative,
please e-mail us at bulksales@mcgraw-hill.com.

This book is printed on acid-free paper.

Contents

Part 1
Finding and Developing Ideas for Writing   1

Worksheets

Friends

School

Out and About

At Your Leisure

Sports and Play

Weird, Strange, and Unbelievable

Part 2
Writing the Draft   111

Worksheets

Part 3
Revision

Worksheets

Part 4
Proofreading

Worksheets

About This Book

Learning to write is a challenging, multiskilled process. Students must learn how to identify, analyze, and develop ideas. They must learn how to compose sentences, build paragraphs, and express ideas within the standards of written English. They must discover their "voice" and learn how to say precisely what they want to say with fluency, clarity, and energy.

Practice Makes Perfect: Mastering Writing can be a valuable resource for developing writing skills. It can be used by both students and teachers. Students (working alone or with their parents) can complete the exercises and worksheets to improve their writing, while teachers will find the materials of the book to be useful for classroom instruction or to supplement their writing program.

The exercises and worksheets in this book provide students with meaningful writing assignments and activities. They will learn how to find and focus ideas for writing; how to write a draft; how to revise their writing; and how to proofread their work. This book, which is based on the stages of the writing process, will give students the practice they need to acquire the skills for effective composition and to grow as young writers.

Learning to write is a difficult task. It is my hope that you will find this book useful in that demanding and rewarding challenge.

How to Use This Book

Practice Makes Perfect: Mastering Writing is divided into four parts that concentrate on writing skills, from developing ideas to proofreading. The book includes exercises and worksheets. An answer key for the worksheets is included at the end of the book.

Part 1 "Finding and Developing Ideas for Writing" begins with the understanding that solid ideas are the foundation of good writing. Ideas are everywhere, and you simply need to learn how to identify and develop ideas for your writing. This part of the book includes information on idea development, six exercises, and a hundred reproducible worksheets designed to help you develop material for writing. The worksheets are broken down into seven sections: "Personally Speaking," "Friends," "School," "Out and About," "At Your Leisure," "Sports and Play," and "Weird, Strange, and Unbelievable." Each worksheet, which serves as a prewriting activity, offers a topic and guidelines you can use to explore and develop the topic.

Part 2 "Writing the Draft" focuses on skills that will help you to write with competence and confidence. Along with information on the characteristics of good writing, fifteen exercises and twenty-two worksheets address topics such as using proper sentence structure; combining and varying sentences; constructing paragraphs; using active constructions, strong verbs, and effective transitions; and choosing a point of view.

Part 3 "Revision" focuses on skills and methods necessary for revising your writing. Three exercises, some "Guidelines for Revision," and twenty-five worksheets are included. Worksheets, which include both fiction and nonfiction, show you the types of weak composition that can slip into your own writing. You are required to identify and revise the weaknesses on the worksheets.

Part 4 "Proofreading" examines the skills and methods necessary for proofreading your writing. Three exercises, some "Guidelines for Proofreading," and twenty-five worksheets are included in this part of the book. The worksheets, both fiction and nonfiction, present you with the errors in mechanics you will find in your own writing. As you find and correct the errors on the worksheets, you will gain the critical skills necessary for proofreading your own work.

Answer Key includes solutions for the worksheets. In cases where answers vary (for example, revision), possible answers are provided.

The worksheets and exercises throughout this book offer nearly two hundred separate activities. They will provide you with a rich variety of writing experiences and help you gain a better understanding of the writing process.

**PRACTICE
MAKES
PERFECT**

Mastering Writing

Finding and Developing Ideas for Writing

Good writing begins with a good idea. Without an interesting idea, even the most skillful writing will result in an unremarkable piece. At best, the reader will plod through such a piece, hoping to find something of value. At worst, he will quickly conclude there is nothing of value and put the piece aside.

Aware of the importance of ideas, professional authors spend great effort and time identifying, developing, researching, analyzing, and organizing ideas before they begin writing. They understand that if they start writing with unclear ideas, they will write with little focus.

This is why it is essential that you learn how to discover and develop ideas for writing. Fresh ideas are the raw materials of which the foundation for clear expression is built.

Discovering Ideas

You have many ideas that can be the foundation of solid writing. But you may not know how to find these ideas. You may not recognize how ideas are interrelated and how an idea can be expanded and refined—and sometimes entirely transformed—into new ideas that become interesting pieces. Through reflection, imagination, and hard work, you can find much to write about. The starting point is personal experience.

Personal Experience: The Source

The seed of every idea takes root in the rich soil of personal experience. From that seed, the idea grows, branches, and, with the right care and nourishment, blossoms and blooms. Not only our direct experiences, but our dreams, things we hear about or learn, and everything that we experience can be the substance of which an idea can be built.

Following are some examples of personal experiences that can generate ideas.

- A nightmare can provide the idea for a horror story.
- Practicing for a piano recital can lead to an article about the sacrifice necessary for achievement.
- Seeing a flyer about a lost dog can generate a story about a missing puppy.
- Learning about global warming can inspire an essay about the importance of conservation.
- Hearing about a hurricane can remind a person about a major storm she experienced and lead to a story of adventure.

You have countless experiences that can serve as ideas for writing. You must access your wealth of experience.

Exercise 1.1 Peering into Personal Experience

Personal experiences—all the things you have ever done, seen, read, or heard about—can lead to ideas for writing.

Think about one of the following topics, or a topic of your own:

- Meaningful Things
- Friends
- Interests and Hobbies
- Things I Enjoy
- Things That Annoy Me

Think of examples that can be included under the topic. For example, under "Interests and Hobbies," you might suggest examples such as reading, skateboarding, soccer, camping, model building, music, dance—obviously, the list can get quite lengthy.

Consider how each can lead to an idea for writing. Here are some possibilities:

- For reading—a review of a favorite book
- For skateboarding—a description of some of the techniques necessary for "extreme" skateboarding
- For camping—a narrative about a fun camping trip
- For music—an article about a concert, or a favorite singer or group

Everyone has personal experiences that can be used to find ideas for writing. Sometimes a personal experience can be developed directly into a topic. Sometimes it can be a spark, igniting the imagination to develop other ideas. Always it is a source of ideas.

The Benefits of Keeping a Journal

An excellent method for tapping into personal experience is to regularly write in a journal. A writing journal is a place where you can express your thoughts and feelings on meaningful topics and issues. In time, a journal can become a warehouse of writing ideas ranging from whimsical musings to deep emotions and concerns.

Writing journals need not be lavish to be purposeful. A composition book or spiral notebook is fine. Always date all entries, because dates provide a time reference that will help you to follow your progress as a writer. Also review your journal periodically to find ideas for writing.

Some possible topics for writing in your journal include: Friends, My Likes, My Dislikes, Responsibility, Home, Family, Things that Bother Me, My Favorites, Pets, I Wonder.

The Benefits of Reading

Reading is another way to tap into personal experience in search of ideas. Reading can present you with new ideas, add information to old ideas, and stimulate reflection on ideas. Reading expands your world and experiences.

The benefits of reading for writing go far beyond expanding your world and experiences. Reading also introduces you to various forms of writing, idea development, and writing techniques. It is no coincidence that just about all writers are readers.

Read as much as you can and as many different kinds of stories and articles as you can. Pay attention to how writers develop their ideas. Note how they build their sentences, how they use description, and how their writing flows.

It is through reading that you learn to recognize good writing. Reading, without question, will help you to become a better writer.

Seeing Life Through the Eyes of a Writer

Most writers view the world with a sharp, critical eye. They see, they think, and they ask themselves "What if . . . ?" To see the world through the eyes of a writer, you must become both an observer and interpreter of life. You must be curious and open to new ideas. You must step outside yourself and look at things from the perspectives of others.

Here is an example. Imagine how your school would appear to a new student from another state. What would be the most striking feature about the school? Would the student feel lost? Out of place? Afraid or anxious? Why might a new student feel this way? Go one step further. Ask yourself how your school would seem to a new student from another country who does not speak English. Considering situations and issues from another's point of view can add to understanding and broaden perspective. It also can lead to new ideas.

Along with viewing things from different perspectives, always look for details, using your senses of sight, hearing, touch, taste, and smell. By paying close attention to your surroundings you can sharpen your powers of observation and learn to see what others overlook.

Here is an example. Imagine you are standing in your yard or a park. What do you see? Trees? What kinds of trees? Big? Small? Evergreen or deciduous? Are the leaves green, or are they painted with the colors of autumn? What about animals? Do you see any birds? What kinds? Sparrows? Robins? Crows? Maybe you see a gray squirrel scampering along a branch. What do you hear? The rustle of leaves? The songs of birds? The barking of a dog in the distance? What does the air smell like? Clean? Fresh? Full of the scent of flowers? If the day is windy, how does the wind feel against your face? Against your body? Is it so strong that it pushes you backward? Is the wind cold? Warm? Humid? What about touch? Maybe the ground is soggy beneath your feet because of the previous night's heavy rain. Or perhaps it is hard because it has not rained in days. What about taste? Maybe you are chewing spearmint-flavored gum (sugarless, of course) that makes your mouth feel fresh. Experience the world through their senses. Awareness of details sharpens perspectives and adds to the images that make up ideas.

Exercise 1.2 Seeing the Details

Select a corner or a part of a room. While sitting, write down as many details as you can about the room. Use as many of your senses as possible, though especially sight and hearing. Remember that sharp, clear details make ideas come alive.

Seeing through the eyes of a writer broadens the world, helping you to become aware of not just the most obvious features of things but the smallest details as well. This is a valuable skill that extends well beyond writing and into all aspects of life.

Focusing Ideas

Once general ideas have been explored, they must be focused. Focusing an idea narrows it down so that you can concentrate on a specific angle. This is important for further development.

Consider the topic *studying*. This is broad and unfocused. Does the topic mean studying in general? Or studying for tests? Or studying a particular subject? The topic does not offer much direction. However, the topic *how to study for math tests* is focused and serves as a clear guide for developing the piece.

A focused topic not only provides you with direction, but also helps you to channel your attention and remain on topic. Focused topics are more likely to result in unified pieces in which all the material of the piece relates to a whole.

Exercise 1.3 Narrowing Ideas Down

Consider the following general topics, or a similar topic of your choosing:

- Fun Activities
- Pets
- Family

These are broad topics that lack focus for writing. Start with one of the topics and write focused examples for it.

Here is an example: Fun activities . . . snowboarding . . . snowboarding at a ski lodge . . . the best snowboarding day of my life. Note how the topics become more focused.

Here is another example: Pets . . . dogs and cats . . . cats . . . kitten . . . bringing my kitten home. Note how the general topics proceed to a specific one, which refers to the time the author brought a kitten home.

Now here is an example using family: Family . . . my mother, father, younger brother . . . younger brother getting into mischief . . . the time my brother drew pictures on his bedroom walls. Notice how the general topics become more focused, leading to the younger brother's budding artistic skills.

These are simple examples, but they show how to focus ideas. A focused idea is easier to write about, because the details are more specific than the details of a general idea.

Developing Ideas

Seldom do ideas for writing burst into a writer's consciousness in complete form. In most cases, ideas are discovered and then must be explored, analyzed, and developed. Through the process of development, ideas may be expanded, refined, or even rejected, only to be brought back in new forms. Sometimes an initial idea gives rise to new ideas that then become the focal point of writing.

One of the best strategies for developing ideas is to consider the five *W*s and *How: Who? What? Where? When? Why? How?* Although each of these questions may not be applicable to every idea, they are useful for most.

Think about a lost gym bag as a basic idea for a story. How might you build a story from this initial idea? Consider using the five w's and how:

- **What?** A gym bag is lost.
- **When?** When was it last seen?
- **Where?** Where was it last seen?
- **Who?** Who are the people in this story? Might one of them have taken the gym bag?
- **Why?** Why was the gym bag lost? Was it simply misplaced? Was it stolen? If yes, why would someone steal it?
- **How?** How was it found? Or perhaps it was not found. In that case, how was the fruitless search conducted?

Using these questions will help you to expand your initial idea and build it into an article or story. Note that the answers to each question lead naturally into more ideas and potentially more questions. The questions serve as a blueprint that will guide you to building a story.

Another strategy for developing ideas is to look for relationships. Nothing exists in isolation. Relationships may not be apparent at first, but everything is connected in some way to something else.

Here is an example. A honeybee visits a flower and takes some of its nectar. The bee returns to the hive, where the nectar is used to make honey. While the bee is on the flower, pollen necessary for plants to reproduce clings to the bee's body. As the bee visits other flowers, some of the pollen rubs off, making the plant's reproduction possible. This relationship is vital to both honeybees and flowers. Mature flowers are important not only for honeybees. They may serve as food for rabbits or deer, be a hiding place for small animals, or simply beautify the countryside or someone's garden. Recognizing relationships between both living and nonliving things is a skill that can serve you well in whatever you do.

Relationships can be complex, but basic ones are easy to grasp—for example, cause and effect (studying leads to better grades), interdependence (animals breathe oxygen and exhale carbon dioxide as a by-product, and plants absorb carbon dioxide and release oxygen as a by-product), and parts to wholes (our solar system is a part of the Milky Way galaxy, which is a part of the universe). Learn to look for and recognize relationships.

Brainstorming is another strategy you can use to develop ideas for writing. A mental exercise in which a person writes down as many ideas as he can about a topic, brainstorming can be a powerful tool to develop ideas. The purpose of brainstorming is to write down as many related ideas about a topic as quickly as possible. Do not pause to analyze ideas during brainstorming, because that only slows the generation of ideas. Evaluation may be done later. Brainstorming is a fast and furious exercise, the purpose of which is to discover and expand ideas.

Exercise 1.5 Brainstorming and Word Webs

Creating a *word web* can help you identify, expand, and develop ideas for writing. Think about the topic "School Lunchroom." (If you prefer, you might use a different topic.)

Think of ideas related to the school lunchroom such as the following: noisy, a break from classes, mystery food, seeing friends, talking with friends, downtime, not enough time to eat, food fights (hopefully not!), and so on. Write down your ideas. Use a line to connect ideas that stem from other ideas. Write quickly and do not pause. The goal of brainstorming is to uncover as many related ideas as possible, thereby expanding the original idea.

When you are done, review the ideas. Some of the ideas on the word web will probably not be used in writing, but others will. Sometimes a web will lead to an entirely new idea that may lead to a new web and more new ideas for writing. Brainstormed word webs can help you flesh out and expand initial ideas that yield fresh possibilities for writing.

Researching is yet another way you can develop ideas for writing. Along with traditional print sources, the Internet provides writers with broad resources for finding information on countless topics. Before the development of the Internet, writers often had to conduct extensive research in order to find information on some topics. Even then, they might not be able to find what they needed. Today, writers often find too much information.

Although researching on the Internet can help you find information, remember that anyone can post information on the World Wide Web. Not all of the information you will find will be valid or useful. To minimize the chances of finding invalid data, conduct research on reputable sites, such as the sites of government agencies, major organizations, and universities. Fortunately, many of the best sites often appear near the beginning of the list that results from a search.

To improve the results of your searches on the Internet, use key terms. Most search engines have become so sophisticated that key terms direct the researchers to sites that they will find useful. The terms you should use for looking up information in an encyclopedia or other reference book will yield accurate results with most Internet search engines. Having a focused topic will help you keep on track during research, and can prevent you from becoming overwhelmed with huge amounts of irrelevant information.

Organizing Ideas

In their enthusiasm (some teachers would call this "rush") to complete their writing, many students want to take their ideas and begin writing immediately. The result is almost always the same: the writers finish pieces that are so disorganized that they do not know how to make improvements. As a result, they do not do much revision. They become dissatisfied with their work, and soon become convinced that they are poor writers.

Organization will help you to clarify and order your ideas, which makes writing any piece easier. Although a detailed outline is needed for some writing, such as research reports, most of your writing will be well served by the basic structure of opening, body, and closing.

Exercise 1.6 Basic Organization for Nonfiction

Think about this simple form for structure.

- **Opening.** One or two paragraphs
- **Body.** One, two, three, or more paragraphs
- **Closing.** One paragraph

The opening should introduce the topic and the problem or situation the writing is about. The body provides information on the topic, including examples and details. Depending on the topic, the body may be one paragraph, several paragraphs, or several pages long. The closing includes a final point related to the main idea or a brief summary of the main idea expressed in the body.

Find examples of this structure in your reading program, social studies book, or science text. It is best to use an article for this activity, as the structure for fiction may not be as clear.

Identify the opening of the article; then the body, including the paragraphs that make it up; and finally the closing. Most nonfiction follows this format. Look for this form in the articles you read.

Worksheets

The following worksheets can help you to develop your writing skills. The one hundred worksheets are divided into seven parts:

- Personally Speaking
- Friends
- School
- Out and About

- At Your Leisure
- Sports and Play
- Weird, Strange, and Unbelievable

The themes of the worksheets in each category are loosely based on the title of the category. For example, the worksheets contained in "Personally Speaking" focus on the author in some way. The worksheets in "Sports and Play" focus on sports or some type of playful activity.

While most of the worksheets are to be developed as articles, narratives, or persuasive pieces, several fiction topics are included throughout the categories. The most fiction appears in the final category, "Weird, Strange, and Unbelievable."

Designed as a prewriting activity, each worksheet will help you develop ideas for writing on a topic. Most of the topics tie into personal experience, making it easier for you to generate material for writing. Because the topics are general, you have much freedom to develop your ideas. For example, with Worksheet 1.4, "Future Gazing," you are given the general idea of considering what you might be like in the future. You can pick a time a year from now, a few years from now, or many years from now. Answering the questions on the worksheet will stimulate your imagination and present possibilities for writing. From that point, you can develop the piece in your own way. For example, you may expand the material through brainstorming and word webs. In some cases, to fully develop your ideas, you may find it helpful to conduct research via print sources or the Internet.

You are to complete the worksheet, using the back of the sheet or an extra sheet of paper if you need more space to answer the questions. After completing the worksheet, expand your ideas and add more details if necessary. The worksheets are guides. You may find that not all the information you supply in response to the questions on the worksheets will wind up in your writing, and that sometimes information not related to the questions will. You may choose a new title that more accurately reflects your writing. Realizing that ideas can be developed in a variety of ways is essential for ideas to flourish. Organize your ideas before writing and follow a basic plan of opening, body, and closing.

The purpose of any prewriting activity is to engage your mind with the writing to be done. Once the process is begun, the only limits are your imagination and enthusiasm.

1.1 An Autobiographical Sketch

Directions: An *autobiography* is a true story that a person writes about himself or herself. An *autobiographical sketch* is a short autobiography. Think about your life. Answer the questions and write an autobiographical sketch. Be sure to include an opening, body, and closing in your writing. Support your ideas with details and examples.

1. When and where were you born? _____

2. Describe your physical traits. (Include such qualities as age, height, color of eyes, hair, and so on.) _____

_____

_____

3. Describe your personality. _____

_____

_____

_____

4. Name three things you like and why you like them. _____

_____

_____

_____

5. Name three things you dislike and why you dislike them. _____

_____

_____

_____

6. If you had to describe yourself in one word, what would that word be? Explain why this word describes you best. _____

_____

_____

1.2 Family Matters

Directions: Think about your family. What makes it special and different from any other family? Answer the questions and write an article about your family. Be sure to include an opening, body, and closing in your writing. Support your ideas with details and examples.

1. Who are the members of your family? _____
   _____

2. Describe the members of your family. (Include physical traits and personalities.) _____
   _____
   _____
   _____
   _____
   _____

3. Explain how your family is special. _____
   _____
   _____
   _____
   _____

4. What do you feel is the best thing about your family? Explain. _____
   _____
   _____
   _____
   _____

1.3 My Pet and Me

Directions: Think about a pet. (If you do not have a pet, imagine that you can have any pet you wish.) Answer the following questions and write an article about your pet. Remember to include an opening, body, and closing in your writing. Support your ideas with details and examples.

1. What kind of pet do you have? _____

2. What is its name? _____

3. Describe your pet's appearance. _____

_____

_____

4. Describe how your pet behaves. _____

_____

_____

_____

5. Describe your pet's favorite place in your home. _____

_____

6. Describe the things your pet likes to do most. _____

_____

7. How do you help care for your pet? _____

_____

_____

_____

1.4 Future Gazing

Directions: Pick a time in the future. This time could be a year from now, a few years from now, or many years from now. Gaze into the future and imagine yourself in that time. Answer the questions and write about yourself in this time period. Be sure to include an opening, body, and closing in your writing. Support your ideas with details and examples.

1. What is the year and where will you be living? _____

2. Describe yourself in the future. In what ways will you have changed? In what ways will you be the same? _____

   _____

   _____

   _____

3. What will you be doing? (For example, will you still be going to school? Will you have a job? What kind?) _____

   _____

   _____

4. Describe your family and friends. _____

   _____

   _____

   _____

5. Describe a problem you face in the future. _____

   _____

6. Describe some good things in the future. _____

   _____

   _____

1.5 Listen Up!

Directions: Think of a time you offered advice to someone—perhaps a friend, sibling, or even your parents. Maybe a friend asked for advice on how to babysit for a neighbor, or your mom needed your help to fix a computer glitch. Answer the questions and write an article explaining the advice you offered. Be sure to use an opening, body, and closing in your writing. Support your ideas with details and examples.

1. To whom did you offer advice? _____

2. What problem did this person have? _____
   _____
   _____

3. Why were you able to offer advice on this subject? _____
   _____
   _____

4. What advice did you offer? _____
   _____
   _____
   _____
   _____

5. Did the person to whom you offered advice take your advice? If yes, did your advice help him or her to solve the problem? Explain how. If the person did not take your advice, explain why. _____
   _____
   _____
   _____

1.6 Lessons

> **Directions:** Think of a time you learned an important lesson. Answer the questions and write a narrative about this experience and what you learned. Remember to include an opening, body, and closing in your writing. Support your ideas with details and examples.

1. What is the subject you are writing about? _____

2. When and where did this happen? _____

3. Who was with you? _____

4. Describe what happened. _____

_____

_____

_____

_____

_____

5. What lesson did you learn? _____

_____

_____

_____

6. Did learning this lesson change you in some way? If yes, how? If not, why not? _____

_____

_____

_____

1.7 Ambition

Directions: Think of your ambitions. What do you most want to achieve? Answer the questions and write an article about your greatest ambition. Be sure to include an opening, body, and closing in your writing. Support your ideas with details and examples.

1. What is your greatest ambition? _____

_____

2. Why do you want to achieve this? _____

_____

_____

3. What must you do to achieve your ambition? _____

_____

_____

_____

_____

4. Describe any obstacles that might stop you from achieving your ambition and how you will overcome them. _____

_____

_____

_____

5. Do you expect to achieve this ambition one day? Explain. _____

_____

_____

_____

1.8 Happy Holidays

> **Directions:** Think about all the holidays you enjoy and decide which one you like best. Answer the questions and write an article about your favorite holiday. Be sure to include an opening, body, and closing in your writing. Support your ideas with details and examples.

1. What are some holidays you enjoy? _____

_____

2. Which one is your favorite? Why? _____

_____

_____

_____

3. With whom do you celebrate this holiday? _____

_____

4. Describe how you celebrate this holiday. _____

_____

_____

_____

_____

_____

5. If you could make this holiday even better, how would you do it?

_____

_____

_____

_____

1.9 Time for a Hero

Directions: Think about a person you consider to be a hero. This person might have lived in the past, or might be living now. Answer the questions and write an article about your hero. Be sure to include an opening, body, and closing in your writing. Support your ideas with details and examples.

1. Describe three qualities a hero must have. _____

_____

_____

_____

_____

2. Who is a hero to you? _____

3. Why do you feel this person is a hero? _____

_____

_____

_____

4. Do other people consider this person to be a hero? Explain. _____

_____

_____

_____

5. Does the world need heroes? Explain. _____

_____

_____

_____

_____

1.10 My Alter Ego

Directions: An *alter ego* is another side of a person that others do not often see. Answer the questions and write an article about your alter ego. Be sure to include an opening, body, and closing in your writing. Support your ideas with details and examples.

1. Describe how you believe others see you. (What kind of person do they consider you to be?) _____

_____

_____

_____

2. Describe your alter ego. _____

_____

_____

3. When does your alter ego most often appear? _____

_____

4. Why does your alter ego appear? _____

_____

5. How do people react to your alter ego? _____

_____

_____

6. What is your opinion of your alter ego? Explain. _____

_____

_____

_____

1.11 Responsibilities

Directions: Think of your responsibilities. Some of your responsibilities might include doing well in school, watching a younger brother or sister, or helping your parents with the chores around the house. Answer the questions and write an article about your responsibilities. Be sure to include an opening, body, and closing in your writing. Support your ideas with details and examples.

1. What are some of your responsibilities? _____

_____

_____

_____

_____

2. Give some examples of how you handle these responsibilities. _____

_____

_____

_____

3. Why are these responsibilities important? _____

_____

_____

_____

_____

4. How do you feel about your responsibilities? _____

_____

_____

_____

1.12 Big Thrill

Directions: Think of a time you took part in or watched an exciting event. Answer the questions and write a narrative about this experience. Be sure to include an opening, body, and closing in your writing. Support your ideas with details and examples.

1. What was the event? _____

2. When and where did it take place? _____

3. Who was with you? _____

_____

4. Describe what happened. _____

_____

_____

_____

_____

_____

5. Why was the event thrilling? _____

_____

_____

_____

6. What was the best part of this thrilling event? Explain. _____

_____

_____

_____

_____

1.13 Admiration

Directions: Think about someone you admire. This person might be living, or might have lived in the past. Answer the questions and write an article about this person. Be sure to include an opening, body, and closing in your writing. Support your ideas with details and examples.

1. Who is the person you admire? _____

2. Describe this person. _____

_____

_____

_____

_____

_____

3. Why do you admire this person? _____

_____

_____

_____

_____

_____

4. How has this person influenced your life? Explain. _____

_____

_____

_____

_____

_____

1.14 Talent

Directions: Everyone has special talents. Think about what you do better than other people. Answer the questions and write about your special talent. Be sure to include an opening, body, and closing in your writing. Support your ideas with details and examples.

1. What is your special talent? _____

_____

2. What skills, knowledge, or ability does this talent require? _____

_____

_____

_____

3. How did you acquire or develop this talent? _____

_____

_____

_____

4. What advice could you give others so that they may develop this talent?

_____

_____

_____

5. How might you improve your special talent? _____

_____

_____

_____

_____

1.15 The Most Meaningful Thing in My Life

Directions: Think about something that holds great meaning for you. Answer the questions and write an article about this meaningful thing in your life. Be sure to use an opening, body, and closing in your writing. Support your ideas with details and examples.

1. What is most meaningful to you? _____

_____

2. Why is this meaningful? _____

_____

_____

_____

_____

_____

3. What do you do to show that this is important to you? _____

_____

_____

_____

_____

_____

4. How would your life be different if this were not a part of your life?

_____

_____

_____

_____

_____

_____

1.16 Friends

Directions: Think about your friends. What makes a person a friend? Answer the questions and write an article explaining what you believe a friend is. Be sure to include an opening, body, and closing in your writing. Support your ideas with details and examples.

1. Describe what you believe a friend is. _____

_____

_____

_____

2. Name three traits every friend should have and give an example of each.

_____

_____

_____

_____

_____

_____

_____

_____

_____

_____

3. Why are friends important? _____

_____

_____

_____

_____

_____

_____

Friends

1.17 Advice for Getting Along

> **Directions:** Think about people you know who get along well with others. Now think about some people who do not get along with others. Answer the questions, then write an article offering advice about how people can get along with others. Be sure to include an opening, body, and closing in your writing. Support your ideas with details and examples.

1. Why is it necessary that people get along? _____

   _____

   _____

   _____

2. What is one thing people should do if they hope to get along with others? Provide an example. _____

   _____

   _____

   _____

3. What is another thing people should do if they hope to get along with others? Provide an example. _____

   _____

   _____

   _____

4. What is a third thing people should do if they hope to get along with others? Provide an example. _____

   _____

   _____

   _____

1.18 Great Times with Friends

1. Who is your friend, or friends? _____

2. Where did you go? _____

3. When did you go? _____

4. Who else was present? _____

_____

5. Describe this great time. What did you do? What happened? _____

_____

_____

_____

_____

_____

6. What was the best part of this great time? _____

_____

7. Why was this time so great? _____

_____

_____

_____

1.19 Adventure Among Friends

Directions: Think about a time when you shared an adventure with a friend or friends. Answer the questions and write a narrative about your adventure. Be sure to include an opening, body, and closing in your writing. Support your ideas with details and examples.

1. Where did this adventure take place? _____

2. When did this adventure take place? _____

3. Who was with you? _____

4. Describe the setting of this adventure. _____

_____

_____

5. Describe what happened. _____

_____

_____

_____

_____

_____

_____

6. How did the adventure end? _____

_____

_____

_____

_____

_____

1.20 When You Need a Friend

1. Who is your friend? _____

2. How long have you been friends? _____

3. When did you help your friend? (Or when did your friend help you?)

_____

4. Why did your friend (or you) need help? _____

_____

_____

5. How was the help given? _____

_____

_____

_____

_____

6. What happened after the help was given? _____

_____

_____

_____

_____

Friends

1.21 Book Tip for a Friend

Directions: Think of a great novel or story you read. Now think of a friend who you believe would enjoy this book. Answer the questions and write a letter to your friend to convince him or her to read this book. Try to show your friend why he or she would like this book, but do not reveal the book's ending.

1. What book would you like your friend to read? _____

2. Who is the author? _____

3. Describe the main characters in the book. _____
_____
_____
_____

4. What is the setting of the story? _____

5. Describe the book's plot (but do not reveal the ending). _____
_____
_____

6. What is the theme, or message, of the book? _____
_____

7. Why did you like this book? _____
_____
_____

8. Why do you think your friend would like this book? _____
_____
_____

1.22 Friendly Character

Directions: Think of some favorite characters in some of your favorite stories or novels. Which of these characters would you most like to have as a friend? Answer the questions, then write an article explaining why this character would make a good friend. Be sure to include an opening, body, and closing in your writing. Support your ideas with details and examples.

1. What is the name of the character you would like to have as a friend?

   _____

2. What is the title of the story where you first "met" this character?

   _____

3. Describe the character. _____

   _____

   _____

   _____

4. Describe the story. (Be sure to mention the setting and plot.) _____

   _____

   _____

   _____

   _____

5. Explain what traits this character has that would

   make him or her a good friend. _____

   _____

   _____

   _____

1.23 Biographical Sketch of a Friend

Directions: A *biography* is a true story of a person's life that is written by another person. A *biographical sketch* is a short biography. Answer the questions and write a biographical sketch of a friend. Be sure to include an opening, body, and closing in your biography. Support your ideas with details and examples.

1. What is the name of your friend? _____

2. When and where was your friend born? _____

3. Describe your friend. _____

_____

_____

4. Describe your friend's family. _____

_____

_____

5. Does your friend have any pets? If so, describe them. _____

_____

6. Describe some things your friend likes. _____

_____

_____

7. Describe some things your friend dislikes. _____

_____

_____

8. What are your friend's plans for the future? _____

_____

_____

_____

Friends

1.24 Trouble

1. What is your friend's name? _____

2. Describe your friend. _____

   _____

   _____

3. Name and describe any other main characters in the story. _____

   _____

   _____

4. Describe the setting of the story. _____

   _____

5. What trouble is your friend in? _____

   _____

   _____

6. How do you help your friend get out of trouble? _____

   _____

   _____

7. Describe the climax of your story. _____

   _____

   _____

   _____

   _____

Friends

1.25 Friends in Opposition

1. What are the names of the main characters in your story? _____
   _____

2. Describe each of the main characters. _____
   _____
   _____

3. Describe the setting of the story. _____
   _____

4. When did the argument occur? _____
   _____

5. What caused the argument? _____
   _____
   _____

6. Describe the argument. _____
   _____

7. How was the argument resolved? _____
   _____
   _____

1.26 What You Need to Know About My School

Directions: Schools around the country are a lot alike. But each is a little different, too. Think about your school. What is it like? Answer the questions and write an article describing your school. Be sure to use an opening, body, and closing in your writing. Support your ideas with details and examples.

1. What is the name of your school? _____

2. In what town and state is your school? _____

3. What grades and about how many students attend your school?

   _____

4. Describe your school (classrooms, gym, cafeteria, computer room, auditorium, and so on). _____

   _____

   _____

   _____

5. Describe the subjects you learn in school. _____

   _____

   _____

6. Describe the extra activities your school offers (sports, music, and special clubs). _____

   _____

   _____

7. Describe a typical school day. _____

   _____

   _____

School

1.27 Improving My School

Directions: An article in which an author writes about a problem or issue and encourages readers to support his or her ideas is an example of *persuasive writing*. Think about the good things in your school. Now think about things that can be improved. Answer the questions and write a persuasive article about how your school can be improved. Be sure to include an opening, body, and closing in your writing. Support your ideas with details and examples.

1. Describe your school (size, number of students, grades, and so on).

_____

_____

_____

2. Describe at least one thing in your school that you feel should be improved. Why should this be improved? _____

_____

_____

_____

_____

_____

3. What could students do to help improve this? _____

_____

4. What could teachers do to help improve this? _____

_____

5. What could parents do to help improve this? _____

_____

School

1.28 School Uniforms: Pro and Con

1. If your school requires students to wear uniforms, describe the uniforms.

_____

_____

_____

2. What are some benefits of wearing uniforms to school? _____

_____

_____

_____

_____

3. Why might students dislike wearing uniforms to school? _____

_____

_____

_____

_____

4. What is your opinion about school uniforms? Explain. _____

_____

_____

_____

_____

School

1.29 Student of the Month

1. What is the name of your award? _____

2. What is the award for? _____

   _____

3. What are the criteria for winning this award? (What will a student have to do to earn this award?) _____

   _____

   _____

   _____

   _____

   _____

4. What will the award be? _____

   _____

5. Who will decide if a student has met the criteria for earning this award? Why is this person (or these persons) a good choice to make this decision?

   _____

   _____

   _____

   _____

School

© Gary Robert Muschla

1.30 Lunchroom Food

1. What kinds of food does your school serve for lunch? _____

   _____

   _____

2. What is your opinion of these foods? _____

   _____

   _____

3. What foods would you like your school to serve for the main part of lunch?
   Why? _____

   _____

   _____

   _____

4. What foods would you like for dessert? Why? _____

   _____

5. What types of beverages would you like served with lunch? Why?

   _____

6. If your school has snack machines that students can use, what types of
   snacks should be offered? Why? _____

   _____

   _____

School

1.31 No (or Yes) to Homework

> **Directions:** Although few students like homework, most receive homework at least a few times each week. Think about how much homework you receive. Answer the questions and write a personal opinion piece explaining your feelings about homework. Remember to include an opening, body, and closing in your writing. Support your ideas with details and examples.

1. Why is homework important? _____

_____

_____

2. When might homework not be important? Explain. _____

_____

_____

3. How much homework do you feel should be given each night? Explain.

_____

_____

4. Do you feel homework should be given on the weekends? Holidays?

   Explain. _____

_____

_____

_____

5. Would it help or hurt students if they never got any homework? Explain.

_____

_____

_____

School

1.32 My Top Picks for Subjects

1. What subjects are you studying this year? _____

_____

2. Which are your favorites? _____

3. Why are these your favorites? _____

_____

_____

_____

_____

_____

4. How might learning these subjects now help you in the future?

_____

_____

_____

5. Do you ever use what you learn in these subjects outside of school?
   Explain. _____

_____

_____

_____

School

1.33 Honor Rolls

1. List reasons why a school should have an honor roll. _____

   _____

   _____

   _____

2. List reasons why a school should not have an honor roll. _____

   _____

   _____

   _____

3. To whom is an honor roll more important—students, teachers, or parents?

   Explain. _____

   _____

   _____

   _____

4. Should your school have an honor roll? Explain. _____

   _____

   _____

   _____

1.34 Physical Description of My Classroom

Directions: Look around your classroom. Notice how things are arranged. Answer the questions and write a description of your classroom. Remember to include an opening, body, and closing in your writing. Be sure to include good details.

1. Start at one corner and look around your classroom. List some of the objects you see. _____

_____

_____

_____

2. Write details of these objects (for example, size, shape, and color).

_____

_____

_____

_____

_____

3. Describe the furniture and how it is arranged. _____

_____

4. Describe any tables and study stations. _____

_____

5. Describe any special items (aquarium, plants, computers, and so on) in your classroom. _____

_____

_____

School

1.35 Special Event

1. What was this event? _____

2. When and where did the event take place? _____

3. Who attended the event? _____

4. Describe the event. _____

_____

_____

_____

_____

5. Describe at least one thing you liked about the event. Why did you like this? _____

_____

_____

6. Describe at least one thing you did not like about the event. Why did you not like this? _____

_____

_____

7. What was your opinion of the event? Explain. _____

_____

_____

1.36 School Greatness

1. What do you feel is great about your school? _____

_____

2. Explain why you feel this is great. _____

_____

_____

_____

3. How has your school achieved this greatness? (Include the efforts of students, teachers, and parents.) _____

_____

_____

_____

_____

4. What does this greatness mean for students? _____

_____

_____

_____

_____

_____

1.37 School Rules

1. Write at least three rules you would make to help your school run smoothly. _____

   _____

   _____

   _____

2. How would these rules help your school run smoothly? _____

   _____

   _____

   _____

   _____

3. Do you think most students would agree that your rules are helpful? Explain. _____

   _____

   _____

   _____

4. What consequences would there be for breaking your rules? Explain.

   _____

   _____

   _____

   _____

School

1.38 New Student

Directions: Imagine that your teacher has chosen you to show a new student around your school. Answer the questions and write a story about this. Include interesting characters, a descriptive setting, an exciting plot, and a climax in your story.

1. Describe the characters in your story. _____

_____

_____

2. How might a new student feel in a new school? Give some examples.

_____

_____

3. To whom would you introduce this new student? Why? _____

_____

_____

4. What places in your school would you show the new student? Why?

_____

_____

5. What (if anything) would you warn the new student about? _____

_____

_____

6. Will the new student like your school? Explain. _____

_____

_____

_____

School

1.39 Perfect School

Directions: Imagine that you have the power to create a perfect school. This school could be everything you would want it to be. Answer the questions and write an article about your perfect school. Be sure to include an opening, body, and closing in your writing. Support your ideas with details and examples.

1. Where would the perfect school be located? Why? _____

_____

2. How long would the school day and the school year be? _____

_____

3. What grades would attend the school? About how many students would

be in each class? _____

4. What subjects would students in this school study? Why would these

subjects be required? _____

_____

_____

5. What special features would the school have? (For example, a big

gymnasium, a swimming pool, tennis courts, computer lab?) _____

_____

6. What would be the most important rule in the school? Why would this be

the most important? _____

_____

7. Would students receive a good education at this school? Explain.

_____

_____

School

1.40 Home Sweet Home

1. Where do you live? _____

2. Describe your neighborhood or the area around your home. _____
_____
_____

3. Describe the climate where you live. _____
_____
_____

4. Describe your home. _____
_____
_____
_____

5. What is special about your home? _____
_____
_____

6. Do you like living here? Why or why not? _____
_____
_____
_____
_____

Out and About

1.41 Round About

1. Describe three places in your city or town (or in the area nearby) that

   visitors might be interested in seeing. _____

   _____

   _____

   _____

   _____

   _____

2. What do you think visitors would like best about your city or town? Why?

   _____

   _____

   _____

   _____

   _____

3. What do you think visitors would like least about your city or town? Why?

   _____

   _____

   _____

   _____

   _____

Out and About

1.42 Customs and Traditions

Directions: Most cities and towns have special customs and traditions. They might have a Founder's Day, a Memorial Day parade, or a fireworks display on the Fourth of July. Think about some of the customs or traditions in the city or town where you live. Answer the questions and write an article about one of them. Be sure to include an opening, body, and closing in your writing. Support your ideas with details and examples.

1. What is a custom or tradition of your city or town? _____

_____

2. How often is this custom or tradition celebrated? _____

3. Where is it celebrated? _____

4. When is it celebrated? _____

5. Who takes an active part in the celebration? _____

_____

_____

6. What, if any, special preparations are made before the celebration?

_____

7. Describe this custom or tradition and its celebration. _____

_____

_____

8. What is your favorite part of this custom or tradition? Explain. _____

_____

_____

Out and About

1.43 Improvements Needed

Directions: Think about how your city or town could be improved. Maybe more parks could be opened. Maybe there could be more activities for kids. Or maybe a public swimming pool could be built. Answer the questions and write an article about how your city or town could be improved. Remember to include an opening, body, and closing in your writing. Support your ideas with details and examples.

1. What is the name of your city or town, and where is it located?

   _____

2. Describe your city or town. _____

   _____

   _____

   _____

   _____

   _____

3. Name at least one thing that can be improved. _____

   _____

4. Why should this be improved? _____

   _____

   _____

   _____

5. How might it be improved? _____

   _____

   _____

   _____

   _____

1.44 Hanging Out

1. Where do you and your friends hang out? _____

2. Describe this place. _____

_____

_____

_____

3. With whom do you usually hang out at this place? _____

_____

4. What do you do there? _____

_____

_____

_____

_____

_____

5. Explain why you hang out there. _____

_____

_____

_____

_____

Out and About

1.45 State of Affairs

1. What is this place? _____

2. Where is this place located? _____

3. When did you visit this place? _____

4. With whom did you go? _____

5. Describe this place. _____

_____

_____

_____

_____

6. Why did you find it interesting? _____

_____

_____

_____

7. Do you think others would find it interesting? Explain. _____

_____

_____

8. Would you like to visit this place again? Explain. _____

_____

_____

1.46 My Special Place

Directions: Most people have a special place they go when they need to be alone, relax, or get "unstressed." This place might be their room, the back porch, or even a treehouse. Answer the questions and write an article about your special place. Be sure to include an opening, body, and closing in your writing. Support your ideas with details and examples.

1. Where is your special place? _____

2. Describe this place. _____

_____

_____

_____

_____

3. When do you go to this place? _____

_____

_____

4. Why do you go there? _____

_____

_____

_____

5. How does this place make you feel? Explain. _____

_____

_____

_____

_____

Out and About

147 Incredible Vacation

1. Where did you go for this vacation? _____

2. When did you go? _____

3. With whom did you go? _____

4. How did you travel to your destination? _____

5. How long was your vacation? _____

6. Describe where you stayed. _____

   _____

   _____

7. Describe the highlights of your vacation. _____

   _____

   _____

   _____

   _____

   _____

8. What was better about this vacation than any other you have taken?

   Explain. _____

   _____

   _____

   _____

148 Travel Firsts

1. What was your travel first? _____

2. When did you first travel in this way, and how old were you? _____
   _____

3. Where did you go? _____

4. Who was with you? _____

5. Describe your feelings about this travel first. _____
   _____
   _____
   _____

6. Describe the trip. _____
   _____
   _____
   _____

7. Have you ever traveled like this again? If so, explain how the other times
   were different from the first. _____
   _____
   _____
   _____

Out and About

1.49 Travel Advice

1. What is your friend's destination? _____

2. Where would you suggest that your friend stay? Why? _____

_____

_____

3. What activities and attractions will your friend find there? _____

_____

4. Which ones would you recommend that your friend try? Why? _____

_____

_____

5. Describe the kind of weather your friend should expect. _____

_____

6. What kinds of clothing should your friend bring? _____

_____

7. What types of equipment should your friend bring? (For example, swimsuit, fishing poles, skis, sunglasses, sunscreen.) _____

_____

8. What would you caution your friend about? Explain. _____

_____

_____

1.50 Travel Calamities

Directions: Have you ever had something go wrong when you were traveling? The car might have broken down. Bad weather might have made your family miss their flight. Or you might have gone sailing and gotten seasick. Imagine going somewhere and everything goes wrong. Answer the questions and write a story about travel calamities. Create interesting characters, a descriptive setting, an exciting plot, and a climax for your story.

1. Name and describe the main characters in your story. _____

_____

_____

_____

2. Where are the characters going? _____

3. Why are they going there? _____

4. How are they traveling? _____

5. Describe things that go wrong. _____

_____

_____

_____

6. How do the characters solve the calamities they face? _____

_____

_____

_____

7. Do they reach their destination on time? Explain. _____

_____

Out and About

1.51 Vacation Mystery

Directions: A *mystery* is a story in which the characters try to solve a crime or figure out a puzzling problem. Mysteries can be as much fun to write as they are to read. Imagine going on vacation only to become involved in a mystery. Answer the questions and write a story about the mystery you must solve. Be sure to create interesting characters, a descriptive setting, an exciting plot, and a climax for your story.

1. Where and when does this story take place? _____

_____

2. Along with yourself, name and describe the main characters in your story.

_____

_____

_____

_____

3. Describe the setting of the story. _____

_____

4. Describe the mystery. _____

_____

_____

5. Describe some clues that help you solve the mystery. _____

_____

_____

6. How do you solve the mystery? _____

_____

_____

1.52 Lost

Directions: Imagine that you or a friend has lost something of value. Answer the questions and write a story about finding what was lost. Be sure to create interesting characters, a descriptive setting, an exciting plot, and a climax for your story.

1. Where and when does this story take place? _____

_____

2. Name and describe the main characters. _____

_____

_____

_____

3. Describe the setting. _____

_____

4. Describe what was lost. _____

_____

5. How did this become lost? _____

_____

_____

6. How do the characters try to find what was lost? _____

_____

_____

7. How do they finally find what was lost? (Or are they unsuccessful?)

_____

_____

Out and About

61

1.53 Strange Happenings

1. Where and when does the story take place? _____

_____

2. Name and describe the main characters. _____

_____

_____

3. Describe the setting. _____

_____

4. What strange things occur? _____

_____

_____

5. What do you do to discover the cause of the strange occurrences?

_____

_____

6. What do you find the cause to be? _____

_____

7. Describe the climax of the story. _____

_____

_____

1.54 Tunes

1. What kind of music do you most like to listen to? _____

2. Describe this kind of music. _____

   _____

   _____

   _____

3. What makes this music different from other kinds of music? _____

   _____

   _____

   _____

4. Is this music popular? Explain. _____

   _____

   _____

5. Which singer or group that performs this music is your favorite? Why?

   _____

   _____

6. Why do you like this type of music? Explain. _____

   _____

   _____

   _____

At Your Leisure

1.55 Star Singers

1. Who is your favorite singer or musical group? _____

_____

2. Is this singer or group popular throughout the country? Explain.

_____

_____

3. What type of music does this singer or group perform? _____

_____

4. What do you feel is the best song of this singer or group? Why do you feel

   this song is the best? _____

_____

_____

5. How is this singer or group different from others? _____

_____

_____

_____

6. Why is this singer or group your favorite? Explain. _____

_____

_____

_____

1.56 What the Song Says to Me

1. What is the title of your favorite song? _____

2. Who wrote and recorded the song? _____

3. What is the song about? _____

   _____

   _____

4. What do you like best about the song? Lyrics? Music? Something else?
   Explain. _____

   _____

   _____

5. Which lyrics do you like the best? Why? _____

   _____

   _____

6. What is the message the songwriter is trying to share? Explain.

   _____

   _____

7. Why do you like this song? Explain. _____

   _____

   _____

1.57 Book Review

1. What is the title of your book? _____

2. Who is the author? _____

3. Who is the publisher and when was the book published? _____

4. What type of book, or genre, is it? (Is it nonfiction or fiction? If fiction, is it fantasy, adventure, history?) _____

5. Explain what the book is about. (For fiction, describe the setting, characters, and plot, but do not tell the ending.) _____

   _____

   _____

   _____

   _____

   _____

6. If your book is fiction, what is its theme? _____

   _____

7. Did you like this book? Explain. _____

   _____

   _____

   _____

1.58 Video Game Review

1. What is the name of this video game? _____

2. For which age levels is it recommended? Is this game suitable for these ages? Explain. _____
   _____

3. Describe the action of the game. _____
   _____
   _____
   _____
   _____

4. What must a player do to win? _____
   _____

5. What strategies can you suggest that will help a player to win?
   _____
   _____
   _____

6. What type of person will probably like this game? Why? _____
   _____
   _____

At Your Leisure

1.59 Favorites

1. What is your favorite thing to do? _____

2. When, where, and with whom (if anyone) do you enjoy this? _____

   _____

   _____

3. Who introduced you to this activity? _____

4. Describe your favorite thing to do. _____

   _____

   _____

   _____

   _____

   _____

   _____

   _____

5. Why is this your favorite thing to do? Explain. _____

   _____

   _____

   _____

   _____

   _____

1.60 Special Day

> **Directions:** Imagine you could spend a day doing anything you wished. What would you do? Answer the questions and write an article about this special day. Remember to include an opening, body, and closing in your writing. Support your ideas with details and examples.

1. Where would you go on this special day? _____

_____

2. With whom (if anyone) would you spend this day? Why? _____

_____

_____

3. Describe all you would do on this special day. _____

_____

_____

_____

_____

_____

_____

_____

4. Why would this day be so special? Explain. _____

_____

_____

_____

_____

_____

_____

At Your Leisure

1.61 Movie Review

1. What is the name of the movie? _____

2. Describe the main characters. _____

   _____

   _____

3. Describe the setting of the movie. _____

   _____

4. Describe the quality of the acting. _____

   _____

5. Summarize the plot of the movie. _____

   _____

   _____

   _____

   _____

6. Describe the best scene. _____

   _____

   _____

7. Would you recommend this movie to your friends? Explain. _____

   _____

1.62 TV Time

1. About how much TV do you watch each day? _____

2. Do you think the amount of TV you watch is too much, just about right, or too little? Explain. _____

_____

3. What types of TV shows do you enjoy the most? Why? _____

_____

_____

_____

4. What types of TV shows do you enjoy the least? Why? _____

_____

_____

_____

5. How might you benefit from watching TV? Explain. _____

_____

_____

6. How might TV watching be detrimental, or harmful, to you? Explain.

_____

_____

_____

At Your Leisure

1.63 Changing Character

1. What is the title of the story? _____

2. What is the name of this character? _____

3. Describe the story. (Include characters, setting, and plot.) _____

   _____

   _____

   _____

   _____

4. Describe this character at the beginning of the story and at the end.

   _____

   _____

5. Describe the changes in this character. _____

   _____

6. What caused these changes? Explain. _____

   _____

7. At the end of the story, was the character a better person? Why or why

   not? _____

   _____

   _____

1.64 Lunchtime Fantasy

Directions: Imagine having lunch with a celebrity or otherwise famous person of your choice. Answer the questions and write about this fantasy lunch. Be sure to include an opening, body, and closing in your writing. Support your ideas with details and examples.

1. With whom would you have lunch? _____

2. Why would you choose this person? _____

   _____

   _____

3. Where would you have lunch? _____

4. What would you have for lunch? _____

   _____

5. If you could ask this person three questions, what would they be? Why would you ask these questions? _____

   _____

   _____

   _____

   _____

6. What do you think the answers would be? _____

   _____

   _____

   _____

   _____

At Your Leisure

1.65 Great Gizmo

1. What is the product? _____

2. Where can people purchase this product? _____

3. Describe the product and what it does. _____

_____

_____

_____

_____

4. How do you benefit from this product? Why are you so satisfied with it?

_____

_____

_____

_____

5. What, if anything, could make this product even better? Explain.

_____

_____

_____

_____

_____

1.66 Changing Places

Directions: Imagine that you and a lead character of one of your favorite stories changed places. You are now the character in the story, and you change the ending. Answer the questions and write a new ending to the story. Create interesting characters, a descriptive setting, an exciting plot, and a climax for the new ending of the story.

1. What is the title of the story you are in? _____

2. Which character did you replace? _____

3. Why did you choose to replace this character? _____

_____

_____

4. Describe the original story. (Include characters, setting, plot, and climax.)

_____

_____

_____

_____

_____

_____

_____

_____

5. Describe the new climax. _____

_____

_____

_____

_____

At Your Leisure

1.67 Funhouse of Fear

1. Where is the funhouse located? _____

2. Name and describe the main characters in your story. _____

_____

_____

3. Describe the setting. _____

_____

4. Describe the funhouse. _____

_____

_____

_____

5. Why were you unable to find your way out? _____

_____

_____

_____

6. How did you finally escape the funhouse? _____

_____

_____

_____

_____

1.68 Games People Play

> **Directions:** Think of a game you like to play. It might be a computer game, a board game, or a card game. Answer the questions and write an article about this game. Be sure to include an opening, body, and closing in your writing. Support your ideas with details and examples.

1. What is the name of this game? _____

2. When did you learn to play this game? _____

3. Who taught you how to play? _____

4. When do you play this game? _____

5. Does the game require teams? Explain. _____

    _____

    _____

6. Describe the game. (Include the object of the game and its basic rules.)

    _____

    _____

    _____

    _____

7. What strategies or techniques can help someone win? _____

    _____

    _____

8. Why do you enjoy this game? Explain. _____

    _____

    _____

1.69 Great Sport

Directions: Think about the sports you enjoy. Answer the questions and write an article about your favorite sport. Remember to include an opening, body, and closing in your writing. Support your ideas with details and examples.

1. What is your favorite sport? _____

2. Which do you enjoy more—playing or watching this sport? Explain.

   _____

   _____

3. If teams are necessary for this sport, how many players are on a team?

   _____

4. Explain what, if any, special positions the team has. _____

   _____

5. Describe the field, court, or playing surface on which this sport is played.

   _____

6. What equipment, if any, is necessary to compete in this sport? _____

   _____

7. Does this sport include a game? If yes, describe the object of the game and how the game is played. (If the sport does not include a game, explain how a person participates in the sport.) _____

   _____

   _____

8. Why do you like this sport? _____

   _____

   _____

1.70 Superstar

Directions: Think of an athlete you admire. This athlete might be a star in a major sport like baseball, tennis, or soccer, or in an extreme sport like skateboarding, snowboarding, or motocross. Answer the questions and write an article about this superstar and his or her sport. Be sure to include an opening, body, and closing in your writing. Support your ideas with details and examples.

1. Who is the superstar athlete? _____

2. In which sport is this person a superstar? _____

3. If this athlete plays on a team, what is the team? What position does he or she play? _____

4. What are this athlete's greatest skills? What makes this person better than others at this sport? _____

_____

_____

_____

_____

5. What tournaments or championships, if any, has this athlete won?

_____

6. What records, if any, has he or she broken? _____

7. What makes this athlete a superstar? _____

_____

_____

_____

_____

1.71 One Fine Day

Directions: Imagine that you could have a day in which you could do whatever you wished. Everything would be perfect. Answer the questions and write about this fine day. Remember to include an opening, body, and closing in your writing. Support your ideas with details and examples.

1. Where would you go on this day? _____

2. Would anyone be with you? If yes, who? Why would you want this person, or people, to be with you? _____

_____

_____

3. Describe the place where you would be. _____

_____

_____

4. What would you do? _____

_____

_____

_____

_____

_____

5. What would make this day perfect? Explain. _____

_____

_____

_____

_____

1.72 Rules for Spectators at Kids' Sports

Directions: Imagine that you could write the rules for how spectators should behave at kids' sporting events. Answer the questions and write an article explaining your rules for spectators. Be sure to include an opening, body, and closing in your writing. Support your ideas with details and examples.

1. How should spectators behave at kids' sporting events? _____

_____

_____

2. What are three rules for spectator behavior? _____

_____

_____

_____

_____

_____

3. Why are these rules important? _____

_____

_____

_____

4. What might happen if people do not practice courtesy and common sense when attending kids' sporting events? Explain. _____

_____

_____

_____

_____

1.73 Being the Best

Directions: Think of a time you were at your best. Maybe you were playing basketball. Maybe you were singing a solo in your school's spring concert. Maybe you were snowboarding down a huge hill. Whatever you were doing, you were at your very best. Answer the questions and write a narrative about this day. Remember to include an opening, body, and closing in your writing. Support your ideas with details and examples.

1. What were you doing when you were at your best? _____
   _____

2. When and where were you at your best? _____

3. Who was with you? _____

4. Describe how you were at your best. _____
   _____
   _____
   _____

5. Why do you think you were at your best? _____
   _____
   _____
   _____

6. Describe how you felt being your best. _____
   _____
   _____
   _____

1.74 Talent or Desire

> **Directions:** Think about participating in sports, playing a musical instrument, dancing, cheerleading, or taking part in some other competitive activity. What is more important to being successful—talent or desire? Answer the questions and write an article about which is more important. Be sure to include an opening, body, and closing in your writing. Support your ideas with details and examples.

1. What must a person do to excel at sports, music, or other activities?

_____

_____

_____

2. Is talent necessary to being successful? Explain. _____

_____

_____

_____

3. Is desire necessary to being successful? Explain. _____

_____

_____

_____

4. Which, talent or desire, is more important? Or are they equally important?

   Explain. _____

_____

_____

_____

_____

1.75 Exciting Event

Directions: Think of a time you were at an exciting event. For example, this might have been a baseball playoff game, a concert starring your favorite singer, or a monster truck show. Answer the questions and write about this event. Remember to include an opening, body, and closing in your writing. Support your ideas with details and examples.

1. What was this event? _____

2. Where and when did it take place? _____

3. Who was with you? _____

4. Describe the event. _____

_____

_____

_____

_____

_____

_____

_____

5. What made this event so exciting? Why? _____

_____

_____

_____

_____

_____

_____

1.76 New Game

Directions: Have you ever invented a game or created new rules for an old game? Answer the questions, then write an article about a new game or a new version of an old game you invented. Remember to include an opening, body, and closing in your writing. Support your ideas with details and examples.

1. What is the name of your new game? _____

2. When did you invent this game? _____

3. Who, if anyone, helped you invent the game? _____

4. What is the object of the game? _____

_____

5. Describe the game and its rules. _____

_____

_____

_____

_____

6. What strategies should a player use if the person hopes to win?

_____

_____

_____

7. Have others played your game? If yes, did they like it? Explain. _____

_____

_____

_____

1.77 Sportsmanship

Directions: Think about sportsmanship and what it means. Answer the questions and write an article about being a good sport. Be sure to include an opening, body, and closing in your writing. Support your ideas with details and examples.

1. What is good sportsmanship? _____
_____
_____

2. Give some examples of good sportsmanship. _____
_____
_____
_____

3. Is being a good sport important? Explain. _____
_____
_____
_____

4. Do you agree or disagree with the following saying? "It's not whether you win or lose, it's how you play the game." Explain. _____
_____
_____
_____
_____
_____
_____
_____

1.78 Consumer Review of a Sports Product

Directions: Think of sports equipment such as running shoes, a baseball glove, or a field hockey stick. Answer the questions, then write an article about a sports product, telling about its strengths and weaknesses. Be sure to include an opening, body, and closing in your writing. Support your ideas with details and examples.

1. What product are you reviewing? _____

2. Why are you qualified to review this product? (What experience do you
   have in using this product?) _____

   _____

3. Describe the product. _____

   _____

   _____

   _____

4. Describe its best features. _____

   _____

   _____

5. How might it be improved? _____

   _____

   _____

6. Would you recommend this product to others? Explain. _____

   _____

   _____

   _____

1.79 Special Activity

Directions: Think of a special activity that you enjoy with family or friends. Maybe you visit amusement parks with your family. Maybe your family has a reunion each year. Or maybe you go to camp every summer with your friends. Answer the questions and write a narrative about your special activity. Remember to include an opening, body, and closing in your writing. Support your ideas with details and examples.

1. What is your special activity? _____

2. Who shares this activity with you? _____

3. Where and when do you enjoy this activity? _____

_____

4. Describe this activity. _____

_____

_____

_____

_____

_____

_____

5. What makes this activity special? Explain. _____

_____

_____

_____

_____

1.80 Competition

Directions: Think of a time you were in a great competition. Maybe you were in a dance competition. Maybe you were playing a challenging computer game. Maybe you were in a tennis tournament. Answer the questions and write a narrative about this competition. Be sure to include an opening, body, and closing in your writing. Support your ideas with details and examples.

1. What was the competition? _____

2. Against whom were you competing? _____

3. When and where was this competition? _____

_____

4. Describe the competition. (Especially note the toughest part.) _____

_____

_____

_____

_____

_____

5. What strategies or techniques did you use to try to win? _____

_____

_____

6. How did you win? Or why did you lose? Explain. _____

_____

_____

_____

1.81 Coach

Directions: Imagine that you are a coach. You might coach soccer, cheerleading, track, or some other activity. What advice could you give to students? Answer the questions and write an article about the advice you would give. Be sure to include an opening, body, and closing in your writing. Support your ideas with details and examples.

1. What sport or activity are you coaching? _____

2. What qualifications do you have to be a coach? (How much experience do you have with this sport or activity?) _____

    _____

    _____

    _____

3. What skills should students have if they want to do well in this sport or activity? _____

    _____

    _____

    _____

4. Is attitude important to being successful in this sport or activity? Explain.

    _____

    _____

5. What advice would you give to younger students who are just starting this sport or activity? _____

    _____

    _____

1.82 Big Game

Directions: Imagine being a sports star and playing in the biggest game of your life. Answer the questions and write a story about this game. Create interesting characters, a descriptive setting, an exciting plot, and a climax for your story.

1. In what game are you playing? _____

2. Name and describe the main characters in the story. _____

_____

_____

_____

3. Describe the setting. _____

_____

_____

4. Describe the plot of the story. _____

_____

_____

_____

_____

_____

_____

5. Describe the climax of the story. _____

_____

_____

_____

1.83 UFOs (Unidentified Flying Objects)

Directions: Many people claim they have seen UFOs and extraterrestrials (beings from other planets). Answer the questions, then write an article sharing your thoughts about UFOs. Be sure to include an opening, body, and closing in your writing. Support your ideas with details and examples.

1. Have you or anyone you know ever seen a UFO? If yes, explain when and where. _____

_____

2. If you have seen a UFO, describe what you saw. _____

_____

_____

3. If you have not seen a UFO, do you believe they exist? Why or why not?

_____

_____

_____

4. Do you believe beings from other planets have visited Earth? Explain.

_____

_____

_____

5. Do you believe that life exists on other planets? Why or why not?

_____

_____

_____

1.84 Inexplicable Occurrence

1. What was the occurrence? _____

2. Where and when did it happen? _____
_____

3. Who was with you? (Or how did you hear about it?) _____
_____

4. Describe what happened. _____
_____
_____
_____
_____
_____

5. How did you, or others, try to explain what happened? _____
_____
_____
_____

6. Why did this event remain unexplained? _____
_____
_____

Weird, Strange, and Unbelievable

1.85 Chilling Nightmare

Directions: Everybody has nightmares. Some nightmares can be so frightening that we wake up in the night shaking and terrified. Answer the questions and write about your most terrifying nightmare. Be sure to include an opening, body, and closing in your writing. Support your ideas with details and examples.

1. What was your nightmare about? _____

_____

2. Who, or what, was in your nightmare? _____

3. Describe the setting of your nightmare. _____

_____

4. Describe what happened in your nightmare. _____

_____

_____

_____

5. Did you wake up during your nightmare? If yes, how did you feel?

_____

_____

6. Were you afraid to go back to sleep after waking up? Why or why not?

_____

_____

7. Why do you think you had this nightmare? _____

_____

_____

1.86 Making Magic

Directions: Imagine being given magic power that will allow you to cast only one spell. Answer the questions and write a story about your magic power and what you do with it. Create interesting characters, a descriptive setting, an exciting plot, and a climax for your story.

1. Describe the main characters in your story. _____

_____

_____

_____

2. Describe the setting. _____

_____

3. How did you receive your magic power? _____

_____

_____

4. What one act of magic did you perform? _____

_____

_____

5. Why did you perform this act? _____

_____

_____

6. What happened after you performed your magic? _____

_____

_____

_____

1.87 Animal Diary

1. What animal is the writer of the diary? _____

2. How does this animal know you? _____

3. Describe what this animal observes throughout the day. _____
   _____
   _____

4. Describe what it hears throughout the day. _____
   _____
   _____

5. Describe what it does most of the day. _____
   _____
   _____

6. What is the best part of this animal's day? _____
   _____

7. What is the worst part of its day? _____
   _____

8. Describe what this animal would say about you in the diary. _____
   _____
   _____

1.88 Historical Reporter

Directions: Imagine that you are a reporter living in the past. You are writing about an important event that happened. Answer the questions and write an article about this event. Be sure to include an opening, body, and closing in your writing. Support your ideas with details and examples.

1. What event are you writing about? _____

2. When and where did this event take place? _____

3. Who was involved in the event? _____
   _____

4. Describe the event. _____
   _____
   _____
   _____
   _____
   _____

5. Why did the event happen? _____
   _____
   _____
   _____

6. What were the results of the event? _____
   _____
   _____
   _____

1.89 Premonition

Directions: Imagine that you wake up one day with a premonition of a coming disaster. Answer the questions and write a story about how you try to prevent this disaster. Create interesting characters, a descriptive setting, an exciting plot, and a climax for your story.

1. Describe the main characters in your story. _____

_____

_____

2. Describe the setting. _____

_____

3. When did you first become aware of the premonition? _____

_____

4. Describe the premonition. _____

_____

5. How did you try to stop the disaster from happening? _____

_____

_____

_____

_____

_____

6. Were you successful? Why or why not? _____

_____

_____

_____

1.90 Extraterrestrial Students

Directions: Imagine that beings from another planet have come to Earth. These extraterrestrials are friendly and wish to learn about us. Some extraterrestrial students are visiting your school, and you have been asked to show them around. Answer the questions and write a story about the extraterrestrials in your school. Create interesting characters, a descriptive setting, a well-defined plot, and a climax for your story.

1. Describe the extraterrestrials who come to your school. _____

   _____

2. Describe the human characters in your story. _____

   _____

3. Describe the setting. _____

   _____

4. Why were you chosen to show the extraterrestrials around? _____

   _____

5. What did you show them? Why did you show them these things?

   _____

   _____

6. What did they find most interesting about your school? Why? _____

   _____

   _____

7. How did other students react to the extraterrestrials? Did their reactions cause tension? Explain. _____

   _____

1.91 Cyberspace Hero

1. What is the name of the game? _____

2. Describe the setting of the game. _____

   _____

3. Describe the main characters in the game. _____

   _____

   _____

4. Describe the object of the game. _____

   _____

5. Describe your attempts to win the game. What strategies did you use?

   _____

   _____

   _____

6. How did your enemies (or opponents) try to stop you? _____

   _____

   _____

7. Did you win the game? Explain. _____

   _____

   _____

   _____

1.92 The Spell

1. Describe the main characters in your story. _____

_____

_____

2. Describe the setting. _____

_____

3. Why did the witch cast a spell on you? _____

_____

_____

4. Describe how the spell got you in trouble. _____

_____

_____

_____

_____

5. How did you manage to break the spell? _____

_____

_____

_____

_____

_____

Weird, Strange, and Unbelievable

1.93 Carnival Coming to Town

1. Describe the main characters in this story. _____

_____

_____

2. Describe the setting. _____

_____

3. Describe the carnival. _____

_____

_____

_____

4. What danger did it pose? _____

_____

_____

5. How did you overcome the danger? _____

_____

_____

_____

_____

_____

Weird, Strange, and Unbelievable

1.94 Big Switch

1. With what plant or animal would you switch places? Why? _____

   _____

   _____

2. Where would you be after switching places? _____

   _____

3. Describe your "new" self. _____

   _____

   _____

4. What would you do? _____

   _____

5. Describe your senses. What you would see, hear, feel, smell, and taste?

   _____

   _____

   _____

   _____

   _____

6. What would be your greatest impression about switching places?

   _____

1.95 The Shoes

Directions: Imagine if you were given a pair of running shoes that made you the fastest runner in the world. Answer the questions and write a story about these super shoes. Create interesting characters, a descriptive setting, an exciting plot, and a climax for your story.

1. Describe the main characters in your story. _____

_____

_____

2. Describe the setting. _____

_____

3. How did you obtain the shoes? _____

_____

_____

4. How did you discover their super speed? _____

_____

_____

5. What did you do after you learned about their speed? _____

_____

_____

_____

_____

6. Do you still have the running shoes? Explain. _____

_____

_____

1.96 Return to the Past

Directions: Imagine being able to go back to the past knowing everything you know now. Answer the questions and write a story about returning to the past. Create interesting characters, a descriptive setting, a well-defined plot, and a climax for your story.

1. Describe the main characters of your story. _____

_____

_____

2. Describe the setting. _____

_____

3. How did you return to the past? _____

_____

4. Describe the past to which you returned. _____

_____

_____

5. You returned to the past with your knowledge of the present. Did you change anything in the past? If so, what? If not, why not? _____

_____

_____

_____

6. How did any changes you made in the past affect the present and perhaps the future? _____

_____

_____

Weird, Strange, and Unbelievable

1.97 The Voice

Directions: Imagine that a stuffed animal, doll, or toy character suddenly began to talk. Answer the questions and write a story about this talking object. Create interesting characters, a descriptive setting, a well-defined plot, and a climax for your story.

1. Describe the main characters, including the talking object, in your story.

_____

_____

2. Describe the setting. _____

_____

3. When did the object begin to talk? _____

4. Why did it talk? _____

_____

5. What did it say? _____

_____

6. What did you do when it began to talk? _____

_____

_____

_____

7. Could anyone else hear the object talk? Why or why not? _____

_____

8. Did the object stop talking? Explain. _____

_____

1.98 Fantastic Pet

1. Describe your fantastic pet. _____

_____

_____

2. Describe the main characters in your story. _____

_____

_____

3. Describe the setting. _____

_____

4. How did you get your fantastic pet? _____

_____

5. Describe an adventure you and your fantastic pet had. _____

_____

_____

_____

_____

_____

_____

_____

_____

Weird, Strange, and Unbelievable

1.99 Mysterious Artifact

Directions: An *artifact* is an object that was produced long ago, such as a very old coin, tool, or ring. Imagine that you are exploring a cave and you find an ancient, mysterious artifact. Answer the questions, then write a story about this artifact and its special powers. Create interesting characters, a descriptive setting, an exciting plot, and a climax for your story.

1. Describe the main characters in your story. _____

_____

_____

2. Describe the setting. _____

_____

3. Describe the artifact you found. _____

_____

4. What are its special powers? _____

_____

5. How did you learn of these powers? _____

_____

6. What happened after you learned of its powers? _____

_____

_____

7. Did you keep the artifact? Or did you return it to the cave so that no one else could find it? Explain. _____

_____

1.100 Super Student

Directions: Imagine that you acquire the power to correctly answer every question your teachers ask. But this power lasts only a day. Answer the questions and write a story about when you were a super student. Create interesting characters, a descriptive setting, a well-defined plot, and a climax for your story.

1. Describe the main characters in your story. _____
   _____
   _____

2. Describe the setting. _____
   _____

3. How do you acquire super student power? _____
   _____

4. How do you feel having this power? _____
   _____

5. Describe what you do with this power. _____
   _____
   _____
   _____

6. Does anyone know about your power? Explain. _____
   _____

7. What happens when your power begins to weaken and you return to
   normal? _____
   _____
   _____

Writing the Draft

The draft is the part of the writing process in which ideas are put into words and onto paper. It is the real work of writing.

Expressing ideas is a big step beyond developing ideas. A first draft is only the first attempt of what may turn out to be many attempts at completing a piece. Few writers get a draft "right" the first time, or the second, or the third. It is not uncommon for professional authors to work through a dozen or more drafts. Even then they may not be fully satisfied that they expressed their ideas in the best way possible. A draft should be considered as but one step forward in the writing process.

For many writers the draft is a time of discovery. Some drafts closely follow the ideas that the writer has already developed. Others lead the writer to new ideas. Some are written quickly with high energy and emotion; others are written in a series of starts and stops because the writer has trouble finding her way. Some surprise the writer with unexpected insights; others are disappointing and force the writer to return to his original ideas to figure out what is wrong. Throughout all this, it is the writer's decisions that ultimately guide the development of the draft.

You should look at a draft as a testing ground where you can examine your ideas and decide whether you are writing exactly what you wish to say. I once had a student who expressed frustration that he had to write four drafts of a story before he was satisfied he had expressed his ideas the best he could. I explained that writing the first three drafts was the only way he could have gotten to the fourth. Rather than viewing reworked drafts as failures, view each draft as an opportunity that leads you closer to the clear expression of ideas.

Without question, writing a draft is work. Writing drafts becomes easier when you understand the fundamentals of sentences and paragraphs. It is upon these fundamentals that effective writing is built.

Sentences: The Foundation of the Draft

To write with competence, you must understand the four types of sentences—*declarative*, *interrogative*, *imperative*, and *exclamatory*—as well as the four sentence structures—*simple*, *compound*, *complex*, and *compound-complex*. Understanding sentence types and structures will help you to write with proficiency and variety.

Exercise 2.1 Types of Sentences

Study the following sample sentences:

- Elena studied for her history test. (declarative)
- Did Kevin complete his science project? (interrogative)
- Close the door. (imperative)
- Look out! (exclamatory)

A declarative sentence is a statement and requires a period. An interrogative sentence is a question and requires a question mark. An imperative sentence is a command and requires a period. An exclamatory sentence expresses great emotion and requires an exclamation point.

Every sentence must contain a subject and a predicate to express a complete thought. In the declarative sentence, *Elena* is the subject and *studied* is the predicate. In the interrogative sentence, *Kevin* is the subject and *did complete* is the predicate. In the imperative sentence, *close* is the predicate and the subject is understood to be *you*, the person to whom the command is directed. *You* (understood) is also the subject of the exclamatory sentence, in which *look* is the predicate.

Write example sentences of your own and identify the subjects and predicates. For additional practice with sentences, do Worksheets 2.1 and 2.2 at the end of this section.

Exercise 2.2 Sentence Structures

Study the following examples of sentence structures:

- Giorgio writes for the school newspaper. (simple)
- Tyrel enjoys baseball, but his sister prefers soccer. (compound)
- When lightning struck a pole on our street, the whole neighborhood lost power. (complex)
- Because it was spring break, Mrs. Jones did not assign homework, but she encouraged her students to continue reading their novels. (compound-complex)

English sentences can take the form of any of these four structures. Understanding these structures will help you to vary your writing.

The first example is a simple sentence. It has one subject, *Giorgio*, and one predicate, *writes*.

The second example is a compound sentence. In a compound sentence, two separate sentences, often referred to as *independent* or *main clauses*, are connected with coordinating conjunctions such as *and*, *but*, *or*, or *nor*. Note the subject, *Tyrel*, and the predicate, *enjoys*, in the first sentence, and the subject, *sister*, and the predicate, *prefers*, in the second. Also note that *but* is a conjunction that connects the sentences.

The third example is a complex sentence. A complex sentence has one *independent clause*, which can stand alone as a simple sentence, and at least one *dependent* (also called *subordinate*) *clause*, which cannot. In the example, "When lightning struck a pole on our street" is the dependent clause, and "the whole neighborhood lost power" is the independent clause.

The final example is a compound-complex sentence. A compound-complex sentence contains two or more independent clauses and one or more dependent clauses. The example contains one dependent clause, "Because it was spring break," and two independent clauses, "Mrs. Jones did not assign homework" and "she encouraged her students to continue reading their novels," connected by the conjunction *but*.

By using all four forms of sentence structures you will be able to vary your writing and present your ideas in an interesting manner. Write some example sentences of your own and identify the structure of each.

Exercise 2.3 Combining and Varying Sentences

Study this example:

> *After school Olivia hurried home. She finished her homework. She went to dance practice.*

These three simple sentences, although written correctly, are flat and boring. Imagine a whole article or story written like this. Short sentences like these can be combined to make writing smoother and more interesting, as in the following example:

> *After school Olivia hurried home, finished her homework, and went to dance practice.*

Here is another example:

> *The sun edged above the horizon. The sky brightened.*

Two simple sentences such as the ones above can often be rewritten as a compound or complex sentence. Combining and rewriting these sentences slightly can result in a noteworthy difference:

> *As the sun edged above the horizon, the sky brightened.*

Combining and varying sentences makes writing more interesting and showcases ideas for readers. For additional practice, do Worksheets 2.3 and 2.4 at the end of this section.

Creating Paragraphs

A well-written paragraph is constructed of sentences related to one main idea. The paragraph contains a topic sentence that states the main idea. Other sentences support the main idea with details and examples.

Although the topic sentence is the first sentence in most paragraphs, it may appear in the middle or at the end of the paragraph. Placing the topic sentence at the beginning of the paragraph makes it easier for most writers to organize the paragraph and provide supporting details.

Paragraphs vary in length, depending on their main idea and supporting details. A paragraph must be long enough to fully develop its main idea.

A major problem with the paragraphs of many young writers is insufficient development. Young writers often use vague main ideas or supporting ideas that lack specific details. To avoid this problem, develop your paragraphs one sentence at a time, starting with the topic sentence. Support the topic sentence with details and examples.

Exercise 2.4 Constructing Paragraphs

Study this example of an obviously undeveloped paragraph:

The movie was great. It had a lot of action, and I liked the performances of the actors. It was the best movie I ever saw.

Although it is clear the writer liked the movie, she offers few supporting details. The absence of supporting ideas undermines the main idea. What kinds of details could be included that would support and strengthen the main idea in this paragraph? Possible details include the following:

- The title of the movie
- The type of movie
- A brief description of the plot and how it helped to make the movie great
- Specific examples of the action
- Descriptions of the characters and the performances of the actors and actresses

In a well-constructed paragraph every sentence supports the main idea. Ideally, even the last sentence of a paragraph should contain an idea that either summarizes or adds a final point to the main idea. The last sentence should then lead into the next paragraph. The effective use of transitional words and phrases helps writing to flow smoothly from one paragraph to the next.

Exercise 2.5 Using Transitions

Consider the following words:

- after
- although
- before
- finally
- instead of
- just as
- rather than

These terms—and others like them—are often used as *transitions* to help writing flow effortlessly from one paragraph to another.

Read the following example:

The snow began falling soon after dinner and continued through the night. By the time Marta went to bed, several inches had already fallen. She figured school would be canceled tomorrow.

Marta played all day in the snow. She and her friends went sledding, built a snowman, and had a snowball fight.

The first paragraph changes abruptly to the second. The change is almost jarring. From Marta figuring school would be canceled the idea switches to playing in the snow. There is no transition. The reader is given no warning of the coming change, the flow is disrupted, and the writing is weakened.

How can this be revised? Here is one possibility:

Just as she had thought, school was canceled, and the next day Marta played. . . .

Note how the words "Just as" and "the next day" make a smooth transition between paragraphs by carrying the idea of school being canceled in the first paragraph over to the second. Find examples of transitions in the materials you read, and use transitions in your writing.

Exercise 2.6 Reviewing Paragraphs

From your reading book, or science or social studies text, choose two or three descriptive paragraphs. (Descriptive paragraphs are best for this exercise because they include details.) Read the paragraphs. For each one identify the topic sentence, main idea, and the supporting details. Pay close attention to the construction of the paragraph, particularly how details support and expand the main idea. Also note examples of smooth transitions, and how they help one paragraph lead into another.

Concentrate on building solid paragraphs in your writing. Organize each paragraph around a main idea, express that idea in a topic sentence, and provide supporting details. For additional practice with paragraphs, do Worksheets 2.5, 2.6, 2.7, and 2.8 at the end of this section.

Showing and Not Telling

Good writers understand that they must show and not tell about ideas if their writing is to have the greatest impact. Because showing requires action, authors who show and avoid merely telling write with sharper and clearer imagery. The difference between telling about an idea and showing the idea through action can be significant.

Exercise 2.7 Show, Don't Tell

To understand the power of showing over telling, study this example:

- After striking out with the bases loaded, Pete's temper flared. (telling)
- After looking at a third strike with the bases loaded, Pete threw his bat down and slammed his helmet to the ground. (showing)

In the first sentence the writer tells that Pete lost control of his temper. In the second sentence, "threw his bat down and slammed his helmet to the ground" shows his temper flaring. Note also that "looking at a third strike" is more specific than simply striking out. Showing provides action that the reader can visualize in his imagination, making the idea clear.

Here is another example:

- The sunset was breathtaking. (telling)
- The sun slipped below the horizon in the bright red sky. (showing)

The second sentence provides action—"The sun slipped below the horizon"—and visual details—"in the bright red sky." The second sentence is an example of stronger writing than the first, because it shows rather than tells.

Write additional examples of your own that demonstrate showing and not telling. In your writing show and not merely tell whenever possible. For more practice, do Worksheet 2.9 at the end of this section.

Using Adjectives and Adverbs Wisely

Many students use too many adjectives and adverbs in their writing. Some overuse these modifiers mistakenly believing that more details will make their writing better. The opposite is true. When overused, adjectives and adverbs weaken writing. Relying too heavily on adjectives and adverbs can distract the writer from choosing distinct nouns and strong verbs. Too many adjectives and adverbs result in wordy expression. Adjectives and adverbs should be used only when necessary.

Following are some examples of overused adjectives and adverbs:

- the evil, wicked, hateful witch (Most readers get the idea with "evil witch.")
- totally surprised (Can someone be partially surprised?)
- the hard granite boulder (Is granite ever soft?)
- completely fooled (A person is either fooled or not fooled.)
- sad frown (Frowns are always sad.)

Adjectives and adverbs must have a purpose in a sentence and must be chosen with care. Instead of bland modifiers, seek ones that provide sharp, distinct details. Even then adjectives and adverbs should be used only when necessary to achieve precise meaning.

To gain an understanding and appreciation of the use of adjectives and adverbs, find examples in your reading. Note how the proper use of adjectives or adverbs can sharpen meaning. For practice using adjectives and adverbs in your writing, do Worksheets 2.10, 2.11, and 2.12 at the end of this section.

Order and Sequence

In real life, things happen in order. All the things we do are part of a sequence of cause and effect. In the same way, articles and stories must be written according to order and sequence. Even stories that include flashbacks follow a plan.

Problems with order usually arise from one of two causes: 1) either the writer is inattentive to order because she wants to finish the writing as quickly as possible or 2) the writer is so enthused with expressing her ideas that attention to order is lost in the heat of writing. Whatever the reason, it must be corrected. Effective writing is based on a sequential development of ideas in an ordered framework.

To gain an understanding of order and sequence, find order and sequence in the stories and articles you read. Especially note how ideas develop logically, how they are related, and how they are usually presented in sequence.

You should concentrate on the order of ideas in your writing. The ideas in most pieces should build from start to end. For most writing, either of two types of organization—a chronological pattern or a logical pattern—provides a practical order.

In a *chronological pattern*, ideas are arranged according to the way they occurred in time. To help you write chronologically, organize your ideas according to time. You might find it helpful to list your ideas. Referring to your list as you write will help you keep to an accurate sequence.

In a *logical pattern*, ideas are arranged according to specific criteria. For example, ideas may be arranged from least to most important, or most to least important. Descriptions may be detailed from outside to inside or inside to outside, top to bottom or bottom to top. A logical organizational pattern may take many forms, as long as the pattern is consistent.

Consider various plans when you are organizing material for writing. Your most important consideration should be to organize your material to present ideas clearly to readers. For practice on order and sequence, do Worksheet 2.13 at the end of this section.

Exercise 2.8 Organizational Plans

Consider the following two organizational plans:

- **Chronological pattern.** According to time. What happens first comes first. What happens second comes next. What happens third comes next, and so on.
- **Logical pattern.** According to specific criteria. Ideas may be arranged in various ways, provided they follow a clear pattern.

Think of ideas that would best be described in each pattern. For example, a narrative of a camping trip should probably be organized in a chronological pattern. An essay about the causes of the Revolutionary War might be best organized in a logical pattern of most to least important factors.

Identify the organization of material you read. Note which you find more often—the chronological pattern or the logical pattern.

Using Active Constructions

Active constructions, sometimes referred to as *active voice*, help to make writing direct and strong. Passive constructions, also known as *passive voice*, make writing indirect and weak. Active constructions are clear and add force to writing. There is nothing vague about an active construction, as the following example shows:

- Taryn scored the winning goal. (active)
- The winning goal was scored by Taryn. (passive)

Notice that the active construction is shorter and provides a clear idea. The passive construction muddles along. In the active construction, *Taryn* is the subject and *scored* is the predicate. There is no confusion that Taryn scored the goal. In the passive construction, *goal* is the subject and the predicate is the phrase *was scored*. *Taryn* becomes the object of the preposition *by*. Most readers easily understand the first sentence, but they may have to think a little about the second. Active constructions are almost always a better choice than passive constructions, because they help readers to visualize action and ideas.

Exercise 2.9 Choosing Active Constructions

Study the following example:

- Jamal kicked a field goal. (active)
- A field goal was kicked by Jamal. (passive)

In the first sentence the action is clear. Although the second sentence says the same thing, it does not express the action as clearly as the first. This is the major difference between active and passive constructions: Active constructions are clear and direct; passive constructions are wordy and less clear.

Here is another example:

- Larissa cuddled the puppy. (active)
- The puppy was cuddled by Larissa. (passive)

Which sentence do you prefer? Most people prefer the first, which is the active construction. For practice with active and passive constructions, do Worksheet 2.14 at the end of this section.

Choosing Strong Verbs

Closely linked to active constructions are strong verbs. Like active constructions, strong verbs paint clear pictures in the imaginations of readers. English is a vast, rich language. We have words for just about everything, and we have precise verbs for all kinds of action.

Exercise 2.10 Strong Verbs

Study the following pairs of sentences:

The wind was blowing hard through the night.
The wind howled through the night.

The squirrel went from branch to branch.
The squirrel scampered from branch to branch.

The little boy cried loudly during his tantrum.
The little boy shrieked during his tantrum.

The second sentence of each pair uses a strong verb to show the action. Strong verbs are clear in the action they express. They result in writing that is less wordy, especially in cases where adverbs are used to support a verb's action. For practice with strong verbs, do Worksheet 2.15 at the end of this section.

Verb Tenses

The tense of a verb shows when something happens, happened, or will happen in a sentence. The three most commonly used tenses are *present*, *past*, and *future*. Other tenses are *present perfect*, *past perfect*, and *future perfect*.

Following are examples of each tense:

- Verbs in the present tense show action that is happening now. For example, *Sandra talks with Lisa each day.*
- Verbs in the past tense show action that has happened. *Sandra talked to Lisa yesterday.*
- Verbs in the future tense show action that will happen. *Sandra will talk to Lisa tomorrow.*
- Verbs in the present perfect tense show action that has been completed in the past and might be continuing in the present. Such verbs require *has* or *have* with the past participle. *Sandra has talked with Lisa.*
- Verbs in the past perfect tense show past action that ended before another past action began. Such verbs require *had* with the past participle. *Sandra had talked with Lisa.*
- Verbs in the future perfect tense show a future action that will have ended before another action begins. Such verbs require *shall have* or *will have* with the past participle. *Sandra will have talked with Lisa.*

Most writers use the past tense more than any other tense because the events they are writing about have already happened. This is especially true for stories and most articles. In some articles, however—for example, essays and editorials—an author may want to convey a feeling that the subject of the article is currently happening. In such cases, the author uses present tense.

You must choose the correct tense for the stories and articles you write. A narrative based on a past event requires the past tense. An article about the lunches currently served in the school cafeteria may best be written in the present tense.

Much of an article that speculates about the end of the current school year should probably be written in the future tense.

Once a tense is chosen, consistency is very important. Pay close attention to the tenses you use to avoid shifting tenses unnecessarily. I have read stories in which students start in the past tense, then switch to the present, only to switch back to the past.

Selecting the wrong tense and unnecessarily shifting tenses make writing confusing for readers. Tense shifts can undermine expression and obscure ideas. For practice with verb tenses, do Worksheet 2.16 at the end of this section.

Subject-Verb Agreement

A subject and verb of a sentence must always agree in number. Singular subjects require the singular form of verbs in the present tense, and plural subjects require the plural form of verbs. In the past tense, except for the verb *be*, the forms of verbs are the same for singular and plural subjects. (In the past tense, the verb *be* assumes either of two forms: *was* or *were*.)

> **Exercise 2.11** Agreement Issues of Subjects and Verbs
>
> **S**tudy the following examples:
>
> - Tina rides the bus to school each day.
> - Tina and Samantha ride the bus to school each day.
> - Tina rode the bus to school yesterday.
> - Tina and Samantha rode the bus to school yesterday.
>
> In the present tense, you must always pay close attention to subject–verb agreement. In the present tense, the singular subject *Tina* requires the singular form of the verb *ride*, which is *rides*, and the plural subjects *Tina* and *Samantha* require the plural form *ride*. When using the past tense, both singular and plural subjects use the same form, *rode*. For additional practice with subject–verb agreement, do Worksheet 2.17 at the end of this section.

Using Point of View Correctly

Point of view (POV) is the perspective an author uses to tell a story or write an article. The two most common points of view are the *first person point of view* and the *third person point of view*. Most writers use one of these two points of view in their writing.

In the first person POV, the author participates in or observes the action. The author tells the story or writes about an event or issue firsthand and refers to himself as *I*. Many writers feel the first person POV is easier to write with because they can use their own voices. It is also easier to write with emotion and feeling in the first person POV, because the writer assumes a role in the piece. The major disadvantage of this POV is the way in which it limits writing, especially for stories. The author, as participant in and narrator of the story, can write only about what she experiences in the story. For example, while writing in the first person POV, the author cannot describe the thoughts or feelings of another character (unless the author reads minds).

In the third person POV, the author writes from a perspective outside the piece. The author is not a part of the action. Characters are referred to as *he* or *she*. The third person POV allows the author broader control of the piece, but the writing may not have the personal feeling of a piece written in the first person. Most writing is done in the third person POV.

Probably the biggest problem students have with POV is consistency. Students may start a story in the first person, switch to third, then switch back to first, only to switch once again to third. Switches between first and third person confuse readers. Stories and articles that suffer from unnecessary POV switches lose focus. Ideas become muddled and writing loses direction.

Some stories use third person multiple POV characters. In such stories, the POV changes from character to character to give readers a different perspective for the story. The POV shifts usually occur at the beginning of scenes or chapters.

Exercise 2.12 Identifying Point of View

Study the following example:

> *I had a busy day. I had two tests in school, had band practice after school, and had to finish my history report after dinner.*

What is the POV in the example? Obviously, it is the first person. Change the POV from the first person to the third person. You might substitute *John* or *Jen* or *he* or *she* for *I*. You would also have to change *my* to *his* or *her*.

To gain an understanding of POV, find examples in your reading and ask yourself why authors chose the POV they did.

As you learn to recognize POV in your reading, you will use it effectively in your writing. For practice with POV, do Worksheets 2.18 and 2.19 at the end of this section.

Using Comparison and Contrast

Comparing and contrasting are tools that help writers to identify similarities and differences. They allow writers to highlight details that clarify ideas.

Comparing identifies similarities and contrasting identifies differences. Use comparison and contrast whenever you need to show how two things or ideas are alike and different.

There are two methods for comparing and contrasting. In the first method, the author describes the first idea fully and then describes the second fully, showing how they are alike and different. In the second method, the author describes one feature of the first idea and compares and contrasts it to the same feature of the second idea. The author then compares and contrasts the second feature, then the third, and so on. Either method helps writers to draw clear distinctions between ideas.

Exercise 2.13 Comparing and Contrasting Pets

Think about the topics "cat" and "dog." To compare and contrast cats and dogs, ask yourself how cats and dogs are alike and different. Some similarities might include the following:

- Both animals are mammals.
- Both are popular as pets.
- As pets they can become "members of the family."

Differences include the following:

- Dogs are more playful; cats like to "do their own thing."
- Cats purr when contented; dogs wag their tails.
- Cats meow; dogs bark.

These are just some possibilities, and it is likely you can come up with more.

Use comparing and contrasting in your own writing. For additional practice with comparison and contrast, do Worksheet 2.20 at the end of this section.

Using Figurative Language

Figurative language can turn average writing into exceptional writing. Figures of speech include *similes*, *metaphors*, and *personification*.

Similes make comparisons using the words *like*, *as*, or *than*. Metaphors make comparisons without using these signal words. Personification gives human qualities to nonhuman things and ideas. The great power of figurative language is in the enrichment of ideas.

Exercise 2.14 The Power of Figures of Speech

Study the following examples of figures of speech:

- The clown's happy grin was like a half moon. (simile)
- Bart's blue eyes were as cold as ice. (simile)
- He was slier than a fox. (simile)
- The fog was a shroud over the valley. (metaphor)
- The birds sang their morning melodies. (personification)

Notice how the comparison or personification of each example is made. Also notice how the figures of speech help readers to visualize the idea expressed by the sentence. Write your own examples of similes, metaphors, and personifications. Ask yourself how the figures of speech enrich the ideas of sentences. For additional practice, do Worksheet 2.21 at the end of this section.

Using Symbols

A *symbol* is something that has meaning beyond itself. Authors employ symbolism to give a character, object, place, or idea greater meaning that it normally has.

Symbolism is found throughout society. For example, a flag is a symbol of a country, a tree may be a symbol for conservation, and a sunrise may be a symbol for a new beginning.

Exercise 2.15 Using Symbolism Effectively

Consider the following symbols:

- Light
- Darkness
- Chain
- Eagle
- Fox

What each might represent? Light, for example, might represent knowledge or wisdom. Darkness might represent evil or trouble. A chain might represent being held back in some way. An eagle might represent power or freedom. A fox might represent slyness.

Use symbolism when appropriate in your writing. For additional practice with symbolism, do Worksheet 2.22 at the end of this section.

Worksheets

For many writers, writing the draft is the most difficult part of the writing process. The worksheets included in this section are designed to give you practice in the techniques and strategies that make writing a draft easier. The skills covered on the worksheets are the foundation of proficient writing. Try to use these skills in your writing. The Answer Key offers possible answers to the worksheets.

2.1 Kinds of Sentences

Directions: Follow the instructions and write examples of the four kinds of sentences. Be sure to use correct end punctuation.

1. Write a declarative sentence using each of the following.

A. eagle _____

_____

B. weather _____

_____

2. Write an interrogative sentence using each of the following.

A. movie _____

_____

B. dinner _____

_____

3. Write an imperative sentence using each of the following.

A. door _____

B. homework _____

4. Write an exclamatory sentence using each of the following.

A. step _____

B. truck _____

2.2 Expanding Sentences

Directions: Expand each sentence by adding words, phrases, or clauses.

1. The wolf howled. _____

_____

2. Riley stubbed his toe. _____

_____

3. Deanna searched everywhere. _____

_____

4. Nikki finished. _____

_____

5. The storm raged. _____

_____

6. Raphael rushed to his bus stop. _____

_____

7. Katie performed. _____

_____

8. The river spilled over its banks. _____

_____

9. Madison waited for her mother. _____

_____

10. Sean grinned. _____

_____

Writing the Draft

2.3 Combining Sentences

Directions: Use *and*, *but*, or *or* to combine and rewrite each pair of sentences. Be sure to eliminate any unnecessary words in your rewritten sentences.

1. Carl mowed the lawn. He trimmed the hedges. _____
_____

2. It rained all day. The soccer game was postponed. _____
_____

3. Maria and Melinda are twins. They don't look much like each other.
_____

4. The evening grew darker. The stars soon appeared. _____
_____

5. Mandy plays soccer. She plays softball, too. _____
_____

6. We might go to a movie. We might go shopping instead. _____
_____

7. Juan had to do his history report. He had to finish his math homework
first. _____
_____

8. The kitten crept up on the toy mouse. It pounced on the mouse.
_____

24 Varying Sentences

1. The sun rose and the morning brightened. (as) *As the sun rose, the morning brightened.*

2. LuAnn finished her science assignment, and then she started her math. (after) _____

3. It snowed heavily all night, and the roads were impassable. (because) _____

4. The power went off last night, and Rob realized he did not have a flashlight. (when) _____

5. Carla had a sprained ankle, but she still went to soccer practice. (even though) _____

6. The sky became overcast, and the rain began. (once) _____

7. Trish was home with a cold, and she finished reading *Dicey's Song*. (while) _____

8. It was the middle of the night, and strange sounds woke Regina. (during) _____

Writing the Draft

2.5 Understanding Paragraphs

Directions: Read the article below. It should be written in five paragraphs (including the first one). Place the symbol ∟ before the first word that starts each paragraph. Explain your reasons for marking the paragraphs on the lines at the bottom of the page.

If you sometimes wonder what the difference is between a meteoroid, meteor, and meteorite, you are not alone. Many people find these words confusing. Meteoroids are rocky chunks of matter that hurtle through space. While many are the size of a small stone, others may be hundreds of feet wide. Most meteoroids orbit the sun and never approach Earth. Some, however, have orbits that intersect the orbit of the Earth. If these meteoroids come too close, they may be captured by the Earth's gravity and pulled into the Earth's atmosphere. Friction with the molecules in the atmosphere will cause the meteoroid to heat up and disintegrate. When a meteoroid begins to burn in the atmosphere, it leaves a streak of light. It is now called a meteor, often mistakenly referred to as a shooting star. Although most meteors disintegrate completely before they hit the ground, some make it through the atmosphere and smash into the Earth. A meteor that hits the Earth is called a meteorite. If a meteor is big, the impact will result in a great explosion and terrible destruction. Fortunately, most meteoroids remain far from the Earth. Of those that enter the atmosphere, most disintegrate long before reaching the ground.

_____

_____

_____

_____

_____

_____

2.6 Writing Topic Sentences

Directions: Read each paragraph, then write a topic sentence for each one. Next, answer the question at the bottom of the page.

1. _____

He looked at the huge pile of books on his desk. His history text, math workbook, and several notebooks waited for him. Leon had so much to do that he didn't know where to start. But he realized that if he was to finish his homework tonight, he had better begin right now.

2. _____

Although he plays many different kinds of video games, Jon likes fantasy games with wizards and brave warriors the best. He enjoys the fantastic settings and action of these games.

3. _____

She sings in her school's chorus and plays flute in the band. She also takes piano and dance lessons. On top of all this, Jenna is teaching herself how to play the guitar.

4. _____

First she looked on her desk. That was where she usually put her homework. But her book report wasn't there. Next Christy checked the family room, thinking she might have left it by the computer. It wasn't there either. About to give up, she remembered she had put the report in her knapsack last night. Now, if she could only find her knapsack.

Choose one of the paragraphs. Explain what clues helped you to decide on the topic sentence.

_____

_____

_____

_____

Writing the Draft

2.7 Using Smooth Transitions

Directions: Write a transition to connect each pair of paragraphs.

1. Marta was running late for school again. She gulped the last of her cereal and finished her glass of orange juice. Grabbing her backpack and calling good-bye to her mom, she rushed out the door.

_____

Relieved she had not missed her bus, Marta climbed aboard and plopped down on the seat.

2. The dark clouds gathering in the western sky looked ominous. Billy began walking faster. As the wind started to gust, he hoped he would get home before the storm arrived.

_____

He ran up the steps to the front door and stepped inside. He was soaked.

3. Roberta read the instructions for installing the new software for her computer. This should be simple enough, she thought. She placed the CD into the drive. Nothing happened.

_____

She examined the CD closely. Flipping it over, she placed it back in the drive.

4. Mark looked at the tools, boxes, and junk that filled Mr. White's garage. There was barely enough room to walk. He frowned, remembering his brother warning him to look inside the garage before telling Mr. White he would clean it out for $20. But he couldn't go back on his word.

_____

He carried out the boxes closest to the door first. As he continued to work, he tried to look on the bright side. He would certainly be done by the end of the week.

2.8 Writing Supporting Details

Directions: Write at least three supporting details for each topic sentence.

1. The darkening sky and growing wind promised a big storm.

_____

_____

_____

_____

2. Caroline hurried about preparing for the surprise party for her parents.

_____

_____

_____

_____

3. Becky enjoyed babysitting Mrs. Hanson's twins.

_____

_____

_____

_____

4. The drought was the worst in years.

_____

_____

_____

_____

Writing the Draft

2.9 Showing and Not Telling

1. Kevin felt miserable with a cold. _Kevin's body ached, his head hurt, and he had been sneezing and coughing all day._

2. It rained hard. _____

   _____

3. Aunt Loretta is always cheerful. _____

   _____

4. Christina is an excellent student. _____

   _____

5. After the heavy rain, the current of the river was strong. _____

   _____

6. Lisa was frightened by the noises outside the front door. _____

   _____

7. Martin is an outstanding basketball player. _____

   _____

8. It was a terrible storm. _____

   _____

Writing the Draft

2.10 Choosing Adjectives

Directions: Complete each sentence by filling in the blank with an adjective. Choose adjectives from the list below that help to paint a distinct picture in the reader's imagination. (Not all of the adjectives will be used; a few may be used in more than one sentence.)

1. The _____ blast of the smoke detector ripped Jimmy from sleep.

2. A _____ moat surrounded the _____ castle.

3. Shari looked at the _____ computer screen and realized her report was lost.

4. All of the campers listened as the _____ man told of the _____ spirits that inhabited the surrounding woods.

5. A _____ oak tree stood at the center of the yard.

6. The _____ kitten pounced on the _____ toy mouse.

7. Jason loves _____ activities such as hiking and rock climbing.

8. The _____ mountains poked into the _____ sky.

9. As he walked home from school, Tim pulled up his collar to block the _____ wind.

10. The _____ sun scorched the desert with heat.

Adjectives

blank	invincible	wintry	playful	blazing	deep
piercing	frightening	cloudless	outdoor	mighty	fluffy
towering	physical	old	exciting	strange	empty

2.11 Choosing Adverbs

1. Travis prepared _____ for the math test and got a perfect score.

2. James _____ is a gentleman.

3. Caitlyn _____ downloaded new virus protection software for her computer.

4. The winds of the storm blew _____ through the night.

5. Nathan's little brother believed the ghost story _____.

6. Kim performed her dance routine _____ at the recital.

7. _____ it would be time to leave for the concert.

8. Not wanting to be late for the start of the movie, Casey ate his dinner _____.

9. Melissa enjoys math and finishes her math homework _____.

10. Jacob double-checked his answers on the test _____ and got every problem right.

Adverbs

recently	often	soon	carelessly	intensely
quickly	always	softly	very	easily
completely	flawlessly	thoroughly	carefully	suddenly

2.12 Writing Descriptions

Directions: Choose a place or thing you know, or create a scene in your imagination. For example, this might be the street in front of your home, a big tree in your backyard, a shopping mall, or a scene in your favorite video game or book. Think of your senses and list words that describe this place, thing, or scene. Then write a descriptive paragraph about your topic.

Place, thing, or scene: _____

1. Sight words: _____

2. Sound words: _____

3. Touch words: _____

4. Smell words: _____

5. Taste words: _____

Paragraph

_____

_____

_____

_____

_____

_____

_____

_____

_____

_____

Writing the Draft

2.13 Understanding the Order of Ideas

1. But she still felt nervous. Kim was nervous and could not stop fidgeting. She took a deep breath to steady herself and assumed her starting position on the floor. When her coach called her name, Kim stepped forward. When Carrie, her friend, tried to assure her that she would do fine, Kim smiled. This was her first gymnastics competition, and she was afraid she would make mistakes and let her team down.

2. He got home from practice around 4:00 P.M. He knew it was going to be an extremely busy day. After dinner Michael did research for his history project. He watched his younger brother until dinner because his parents had not yet returned from shopping. That morning, he helped his father mow the lawn and trim the hedges. By the time Michael went to sleep that night, he was exhausted. Michael woke up early on Saturday. Right after lunch Michael went to soccer practice.

2.14 Using Active Constructions

1. The Frisbee was caught by David. *David caught the Frisbee.*

2. The great oak tree was uprooted by the wind. _____

   _____

3. The art club's new logo was designed by Megan. _____

   _____

4. The debate was won by Trish. _____

   _____

5. The car was washed by Tony. _____

   _____

6. A violin solo in the eighth-grade winter concert was played by Marissa.

   _____

7. The unsuspecting rabbit was crept up on by the fox. _____

   _____

8. Treacherous whiteout conditions were caused by the intense snowstorm.

   _____

9. *The Slave Dancer* was written by Paula Fox. _____

   _____

10. Homework for the spring break was assigned by Mrs. Carter. _____

    _____

Writing the Draft

2.15 Using Strong Verbs

1. The little boy quickly took the wrapping paper off his birthday present.

   The little boy ripped the wrapping paper off his birthday present.

2. The hawk was high over the field in search of prey. _____

   _____

3. The cat walked quietly toward the bird. _____

   _____

4. The girls talked softly in the library. _____

   _____

5. Joanna moved quickly out of the way of the speeding car. _____

   _____

6. The little boy cried loudly when he stubbed his toe. _____

   _____

7. Thomas went hurriedly to catch the bus before it pulled away.

   _____

8. Alvaro ran very fast to the finish line. _____

   _____

9. The cold winter wind blew intensely across the open field. _____

   _____

10. The fog was entirely over the valley. _____

    _____

Writing the Draft

2.16 Using Verb Tenses Correctly

Directions: Identify the tense used in each of the following sentences—present, past, future, present perfect, past perfect, or future perfect.

1. Liz babysits her neighbor's little girl each day after school. _____

2. Paulo will have finished reading his novel by Friday. _____

3. Michael is a great musician. _____

4. Alison walked to the park with Monica this morning. _____

5. Matt has called about the lost tickets several times. _____

6. The ventriloquist will be the final act in the show. _____

7. The dog chased the cat up a tree. _____

8. Lee Ann had asked to be excused from last week's meeting. _____

9. Bobby will study for his history test after dinner. _____

10. I predict the Cougars will win the championship by ten points.

_____

Write a sentence of your own for each of the six tenses of verbs.

1. _____

2. _____

3. _____

4. _____

5. _____

6. _____

Writing the Draft

2.17 Making Sure Subjects and Verbs Agree

> **Directions:** Complete each sentence by writing the correct form of a verb. Choose the verbs from the bottom of the page. Each verb should be used only once. (Remember to use the correct form of each verb.)

1. Tia _____ the best chocolate cake I have ever tasted.

2. Alexis _____ her cell phone for making calls, taking pictures, and connecting to the Internet.

3. Most kids of middle school age _____ far too much TV each day.

4. Jannie and Kim _____ several times each week to keep physically fit.

5. A family of raccoons _____ in a big tree behind our house.

6. Mark _____ football, basketball, and baseball for our school.

7. Lena _____ her younger sister with homework every evening after dinner.

8. The members of the jazz band _____ the drums each morning before classes begin.

9. Stars _____ the brightest on clear winter nights.

10. After every heavy rain the river behind the soccer fields _____ above its banks.

Verbs

play	twinkle	bake	rise	help
jog	use	watch	live	practice

2.18 Understanding First Person Point of View

Danny sighed, thinking of all the math and science homework he had to do. He also had to read another chapter in his novel.

He looked at the pile of books on his desk and frowned. He couldn't decide which book to open first, but he knew he had better start if he wanted to meet his friends later.

Danny opened his math book and began. After he finished ten word problems, he answered his science questions. Finally he read the chapter in his novel.

As soon as he was done, Danny went to see his friends, who were waiting for him at the basketball court. By the time he arrived, they had already chosen teams. They had saved a spot for Danny.

_____

_____

_____

_____

_____

_____

_____

_____

_____

_____

_____

_____

_____

_____

Writing the Draft

2.19 Understanding Third Person Point of View

I woke up early on the Saturday of the five-kilometer race. My father and I would be running to help raise money for charity. I had been jogging with him four times a week for the last several weeks, and I was certain I would finish the race.

Once the race began, though, I wasn't so sure. There were a lot of hills, and we were running into the wind. I began to worry that I would become tired and have to walk to the finish line.

Remembering my father's advice about keeping a slow but steady pace, I kept going. When at last I saw the finish line, I smiled and sprinted the last hundred yards.

I didn't win any trophy. But that was OK. I was satisfied simply having run and finished my first big race.

_____

_____

_____

_____

_____

_____

_____

_____

_____

_____

_____

_____

_____

2.20 Using Comparison and Contrast

Directions: Read the article about African elephants and Indian elephants. List how they are alike and different.

The elephant is the largest living land mammal on Earth. There are two species of elephants: the African elephant and the Indian elephant. Both elephants have trunks and eat mostly grass and leaves. But there are important differences between the two.

The African elephant is found primarily in the tropical forests and grasslands of Africa. It is the larger of the two kinds of elephants and can reach a height of thirteen feet. It is tallest at the shoulder. The African elephant also has larger ears, which may reach a length of five feet from top to bottom. The skin of an African elephant is more wrinkled than the skin of an Indian elephant. Both male and female African elephants have tusks.

The Indian elephant is found in India and Southeast Asia. It is usually smaller than the African elephant and is tallest at the arch of the back. Only male Indian elephants have tusks.

Compare
How the African elephant and Indian elephant are alike:

_____

_____

_____

_____

Contrast
How the African elephant and Indian elephant are different:

_____

_____

_____

_____

Writing the Draft

2.21 Using Figures of Speech

1. eagle: _____

_____

2. thief: _____

_____

3. rocket: _____

_____

Write a sentence that includes a metaphor for each of the following.

4. alarm: _____

_____

5. shark: _____

_____

6. flowers: _____

_____

Write a sentence that includes a personification for each of the following.

7. fireflies: _____

_____

8. sky: _____

_____

2.22 Using the Power of Symbolism

Directions: Match the symbol with the idea it could represent. Write the idea on the line after the symbol.

1. door _____   a beginning

2. fire _____   a journey

3. wall _____   slyness

4. darkness _____   a passageway or opening

5. dawn _____   wisdom

6. owl _____   sadness, worry, concern

7. ship _____   knowledge, enlightenment

8. circle _____   infinity, endlessness

9. night _____   obstacle, hindrance

10. fox _____   end, finish

Choose one of the symbols above (or one of your own) and write a paragraph showing how the symbol can be used.

_____

_____

_____

_____

_____

_____

Writing the Draft

Revision

R evision is the stage of the writing process in which an author reworks, refines, and finalizes her ideas. It is a time of "re-seeing" what she has written and making it better.

Revision is essential for improving writing. It is critical for making writing as clear and meaningful to readers as possible. For most authors, it is solid revision that leads to the successful expression of ideas. It is through revision that authors achieve their best work.

What Is Revision?

In its broadest sense, revision includes any activity that makes a draft better. In its narrowest, it is replacing one word with another because the second word better communicates what the author wants to say. Note that editing of mechanics—capitalization and punctuation, for example—also occurs during revision. But revision should not be confused with proofreading, the primary purpose of which is to correct errors in mechanics (see Part 4, "Proofreading").

Revision includes a variety of activities. As you revise your writing, you may be engaged in any of the following:

- Rereading
- Rewriting
- Reviewing
- Rethinking
- Rearranging
- Restructuring
- Tightening
- Deleting
- Moving
- Expanding
- Unifying

- Correcting
- Redrafting
- Checking

Writing is not finished until it has been revised. All professional writers revise their work. During an interview for the *Paris Review*, Ernest Hemingway said that he rewrote the last page of his book *A Farewell to Arms* thirty-nine times before he was satisfied with his work. Hemingway's example illustrates the seriousness with which professional authors undertake the task of revision. They know that their finest writing takes form during revision.

Skills in Revision

Revision is detailed, demanding work. Not only must the writer work to improve specifics—for example, select the best words to express an idea clearly and smoothly—he must also work to improve the piece as a whole. Moreover, each piece is different and has different strengths and weaknesses. For most authors, revision is a process that is a mix of art, craft, and effort.

Although just about every article or story benefits from revision, the amount and type of revision vary. Some pieces require much revision. Maybe the writer drifted off the topic, maybe he did not provide enough information to explain his ideas, or maybe his organization was weak. Perhaps his use of metaphors was lacking, or he used too many weak verbs and passive constructions. In other cases, a piece might require only some tightening and minor rewriting. An author's first task during revision is to recognize what needs to be reworked and what does not.

Being able to recognize what needs to be revised requires a grasp of the fundamentals of effective writing (which were discussed in Part 2, "Writing the Draft"). The following elements are important to any piece and will provide you with direction as you revise your writing.

- Effective, logical organization
- Basic structure of opening, body, and closing
- Well-constructed paragraphs
- Main ideas and supporting details and examples
- Varied sentence structure
- Agreement of subjects and verbs
- Active constructions
- Strong verbs
- Showing and not telling
- Consistent tenses
- Consistent point of view
- Smooth flow and effective transitions
- Figurative language
- Symbolism

Revision can be both puzzling and frustrating. It is an individual process, based on your purpose for the piece. It is your responsibility as an author. When you revise your own work, you grow as a writer.

A Plan for Revision

Because revision has so many elements, there can be no firm, set procedure for revising your writing. As you gain experience with revision, you will eventually develop your own methods. But this takes time. Practice leads to proficiency.

A good plan to follow is to begin revising from the perspective of the overall piece and work down to the details. This plan provides direction and will help you to focus on specific elements at different points in the revision process.

Begin by reading through the piece and concentrating on unity. *Unity* is a broad term that can be used to include all aspects of a piece. In an article or story that demonstrates unity, all parts work together to create effective expression. All main ideas and supporting details relate to the topic. Everything moves the piece forward in support of the author's purpose and theme. For example, an article about how to study for tests that drifts and includes information about the pleasure of reading would suffer from a lack of unity. It would prove to be confusing to readers, who expect to learn about test-taking strategies and not about reading for enjoyment. To achieve unity, any material not essential to the topic should be deleted.

The style of writing, including the use of figures of speech and symbolism, also contributes to unity. Style helps to determine the mood of a piece. For example, a horror story should be written in a dark, foreboding style, which can result in a suspenseful mood. A humorous essay should be written in an easy style that generates a lighthearted mood. A style that does not suit the topic weakens the impact of the writer's ideas.

After you have made certain that all parts of the piece belong, and that your writing shows unity, read through the piece again and concentrate on the overall structure. There should be a solid opening, logical development through the body, and a strong closing. The introduction should lead into the body, and the body should lead into the closing. Paragraphs should be used to develop main ideas, and main ideas should be supported with details and examples. The various parts of the piece should be in balance. Ideas of equal importance should be given equal weight. Ideas of lesser importance should be given less weight. All parts of the piece should complement each other.

Next, focus on consistency of tense. Throughout the piece, all tenses should be consistent and appropriate. For example, a story should be written in the past tense. An essay, however, might be written in the present. Any unnecessary shifts in tense should be corrected.

Point of view must be consistent as well. If a story is started in the first person point of view, it should continue in the first person. Likewise, if a story is begun in the third person point of view, it should remain in the third person. Switching from first to third person point of view weakens a piece.

After focusing on general consistency, concentrate on individual paragraphs, sentences, phrases, and words. Again, eliminate anything that does not belong. Strive to make sure that every paragraph has a topic sentence and sufficient details. In addition, vary and combine sentences, make certain that subjects and verbs agree, rely on active constructions, and select just the right words to express ideas. Transitions should be smooth. Figures of speech—similes, metaphors, and personification—and symbolism should be appropriate for the topic and support expression. Now is the time to make writing the best it can be.

As you gain experience and confidence in revision, you will come to see revision as a satisfying part of the writing process. Revision will help you make certain that your writing expresses exactly what you wish to say.

Exercise 3.1 A Revision Plan

The following steps can help you revise your writing:

1. Read the entire piece and focus on unity—all parts should relate to the whole.
2. Focus on writing style—make sure it creates the right mood for the topic.
3. Focus on structure—opening, body, and closing. Main ideas should be developed with details and examples.
4. Focus on consistency of tense.
5. Focus on consistency of point of view.
6. Focus on individual paragraphs, sentences, phrases, and words—all should help to express ideas clearly.

Revision often requires rereading and reworking writing several times. Following a basic plan that concentrates on looking at the overall piece and working down through the details can be a helpful strategy.

Exercise 3.2 Recognizing Good Writing

Recognizing good writing of others is a major step in revising your own writing. Use articles and stories from your texts as examples. Read the material and note the unity, how everything in the article or story relates to the topic and the author's purpose. Note the organization of the piece and how the structure displays ideas in a logical manner. Notice the style and how it augments the piece. Recognize the use of consistent tenses and point of view. Examine how the author varied her sentences, used active constructions, relied on strong verbs, and achieved a smooth flow of ideas through effective transitions.

Good writing is almost always a result of good revision. Revision is your opportunity to make your writing as clear and interesting as possible for your readers. This is the time to put ideas into their final shape.

Revision Peer Consultants

One of the hardest parts of revision is recognizing writing that is not wrong but that could be improved. I once had a student ask me, "How do you know when to stop revising?" This was an excellent question, for which the only answer is, "When you are convinced the material is as strong and clear as you can make it."

Because you may not be sure what to revise, you may find revision to be a difficult part of the writing process. It is hard to step back far enough from your writing to be objective and see the weaknesses in your material.

Sometimes consulting with a partner can help. You and a partner can read each other's work and offer suggestions for revision. You should not correct the papers. Instead, you should underline items you feel should be revised and write comments in the margins. The author can then consider the places his partner identified for revision. The more practice you have with revision, the more comfortable and confident you will become with the process.

Exercise 3.3 Revision Consultants

Work with a partner on revision. You and your partner are to act as revision consultants. You are to read each other's writing and identify instances where you feel revision could improve the piece. Underline where revision might be necessary on your partner's paper. Write brief comments in the adjacent margins. For example, a spot where a stronger verb could be used ("screamed" instead of "cried out hysterically") might be identified and labeled "Use stronger verb." The consultant should not make the revision; this work should be left to the author.

The writer either agrees or disagrees with the consultant's findings. If she agrees that revision is necessary, she may offer possibilities for revising the material and seek the input of her partner. She would then go on to revise the material. If she disagrees, she should offer a reason why she feels revision in this instance is unnecessary.

Learning how to revise efficiently and effectively takes a long time and requires a major effort. These efforts are well worth undertaking because revision provides the opportunity to create quality material. It is through revision that you will truly emerge as a writer.

Worksheets

Revision is a difficult activity. The worksheets included in this section are designed to provide you with practice in revision.

The worksheets, which include both articles and stories, cover a variety of topics. You will find the worksheets challenging in that much of the material that should be revised is not technically wrong, but definitely could be improved. The exceptions are run-on sentences, fragments, unnecessary shifts in tense, faulty point of view, and errors in subject–verb agreement.

The "Guidelines for Revision" on page 155 offer direction for revising. Remember that most articles and stories can be revised in various manners, depending on the material and purpose as well as the background and outlook of the writer.

The worksheets proceed from relatively basic to more challenging. The directions for Worksheets 3.1 through 3.13 focus on specific elements to revise, while Worksheets 3.14 through 3.25 do not provide any hints of what weaknesses to look for. Each worksheet has several items that could be revised. Since revised articles and stories will vary, the Answer Key (page 211) offers a possible revision of each worksheet.

Work hard to revise your writing. It is through revision that you will achieve your best writing.

Guidelines for Revision

Asking yourself the following questions can help you revise your writing.

1. Is my topic focused?

2. Is my writing unified? Do all of my ideas and details relate to my topic?

3. Is my organization logical and clear? Does my writing have an opening, body, and closing?

4. Does each paragraph have a main idea? Have I supported each main idea with details and examples?

5. Does my writing style fit my topic?

6. Have I varied my sentence construction?

7. Have I used active rather than passive constructions?

8. Have I used strong verbs?

9. Do my subjects and verbs agree?

10. Did I show and not tell?

11. Are my tenses consistent?

12. Is my point of view consistent?

13. Does my writing flow smoothly? Have I used effective transitions?

14. Have I deleted all unnecessary information and words?

15. Have I said what I want to say and expressed my ideas clearly?

3.1 Hot Springs and Geysers

Directions: Revise the article and make any changes you feel will improve it. Be sure it has an opening, body, and closing. Organize the article into paragraphs and eliminate any unnecessary information. Rewrite the revised article on a separate sheet of paper.

A hot spring is water that flows out of the ground at temperatures higher than the air temperature. Most hot springs result from underground water flowing over molten or very hot rock. The rock heats the water. Sometimes the molten rock, which is very extremely hot, can heat the water to such high temperatures that the water turns to steam. If the pressure increases enough, steam and water are pushed toward the surface with great force. The steam and water may spout high into the air. This eruption of steam and water is called a geyser. Most geysers are found in three parts of the world. These three parts of the world are the western United States, Iceland, and New Zealand. The most famous geyser in the world is Old Faithful in Yellowstone National Park. Most geysers erupt at irregular intervals. But this geyser, Old Faithful, erupts on average once every ninety-four minutes each day. Several thousand gallons of hot water shoot up to 170 feet in the air. Watching a geyser is a thrilling experience. It is very exciting to watch a geyser erupt. Geysers are one of nature's most exciting spectacles.

3.2 Comets

Comets may be thought of as being big, dirty snowballs in space. Scientists believe that most comets are made up of about 75 percent ice and 25 percent dust and rock. When a comet approaches the sun, the heat from the sun causes some of the ice to vaporize. It glows then. As the comet gets closer to the sun, radiation, called the solar wind, sweeps the vaporizing gases away from the comet. The sun is an average star. This produces a tail. Because of the solar wind, which is really radiation, the tail of a comet always streaks away from the sun. No one knows for certain how comets originated. But many scientists believe comets are leftover matter from the time our solar system formed. They do not know how many comets are in our solar system. While most comets remain very, very far from Earth, some have hit our planet. A comet impact is thought to have caused a great explosion in Siberia in 1908. Fortunately, comet impacts are rare. In the past, people looked at comets as evil omens. They thought that comets brought wars, plagues, and death. Today people look at comets with interest and curiosity. They know that comets are just simply dirty snowballs in our solar system.

Revision

3.3 Early History of the Roller Coaster

Directions: Revise the article and make any changes you feel will improve it. Be sure it has an opening, body, and closing. Organize the article into paragraphs and eliminate any unnecessary information. Rewrite the revised article on a separate sheet of paper.

The origin of the modern roller coaster can be traced to Russian ice slides of the seventeenth century. The slides were first built in the mid-1600s in the area around present-day St. Petersburg. St. Petersburg is an important Russian city. The ice slides were large wooden structures. Some were between seventy and eighty feet high. During the winters the slides were enjoyed by a lot of people, including royalty. The slides were covered with ice several inches thick. Large sleds sped down a steep drop that extended hundreds of feet. Stairs were constructed at the backs of the slides for riders to walk up to the top. Some historians believe the Russians also built the first true roller coaster. This first real coaster was a carriage with wheels that ran along a track. There is little evidence. But supposedly it was built in St. Petersburg. This was in the late 1700s. Other historians, however, believe the French built the first coasters with wheels in the early 1800s. Records indicate that two coasters with wheels that locked onto tracks were operating in France around 1817. From these simple and basic designs, the great roller coasters of today have evolved and have become a reality. Roller coaster fans can only wonder what thrills the coasters of tomorrow will provide.

3.4 Louis Pasteur and the Vaccine for Rabies

Directions: Revise the article and make any changes you feel will improve it. Especially pay attention to logical development. Eliminate any unnecessary information or words. Rewrite the revised article on a separate sheet of paper.

Louis Pasteur (1822–1895) was a great French scientist. One of his many important discoveries was a vaccine for rabies. Pasteur also helped to prove that germs cause disease.

Rabies is an awful, frightening, terrible infection of the nervous system. To become infected, a person or animal must be bitten by an animal that already has the disease. The disease can infect all warm-blooded animals. Before Pasteur's vaccine, the terrible disease called rabies almost always was fatal. It is caused by a virus.

One day a mother brought her nine-year-old son to Pasteur's laboratory. This was in 1885, and Pasteur was working on a vaccine for rabies. Without the vaccine the boy would surely die, because the boy had been bitten by a rabid dog. But the vaccine had not been tested yet on humans. No one knew if it would work. Pasteur agreed to try his vaccine. The boy survived and stayed healthy. The vaccine was successful. A vaccine for rabies had been found.

Since then, thousands of people have been saved from rabies by Pasteur's vaccine. Today, dogs and cats are immunized to prevent them from getting the disease and infecting people.

Revision

3.5 Benefits of Regular Exercise

Directions: Revise the article and make any changes you feel will improve it. Especially pay attention to varying sentence structure and subject–verb agreement. Rewrite the revised article on a separate sheet of paper.

A plan of regular exercise is vital for good health. Regular exercise cause you to breathe more deeply. It makes your heart pump more vigorously. It makes your muscles work harder. It makes your body use more calories. It helps to keep your body at a healthy weight.

Exercising as little as thirty minutes a day can keep your body fit. You should exercise four or five times per week. Regular exercise can also help you think better. It can help you sleep better. It can help you feel better. It benefits your entire body.

You can exercise in various ways. You can walk. You can jog. You can play sports. You can work out in a gym. You can ride your bike. You can skate. You can swim. You can dance. Any activity that make your heart beat faster for a sustained length of time is beneficial.

Exercise is necessary for your health. You should design a practical exercise plan that fit in with your daily schedule.

Revision

3.6 Whale Shark

Directions: Revise the article and make any changes you feel will improve it. Especially pay attention to unity, sentence structure, and subject–verb agreement. Eliminate any unnecessary information. Rewrite the revised article on a separate sheet of paper.

Despite its name, the whale shark is not related to whales at all. Whales are mammals, and sharks are fish. The whale shark are the largest known fish. It may grow to a length of fifty feet. And weigh more than twenty tons. This account for the "whale" part of its name.

Whale sharks are not related to dolphins, either. Dolphins, which are relatives of whales, are mammals.

Whale sharks are found in tropical waters. Around the world. Most of the time they remain in the open sea. They are sighted sometimes near the shore. They are usually solitary creatures. Sometimes they are sighted in schools of dozens or hundreds of individuals.

Whale sharks are known as filter-feeding fish. When feeding, a whale shark swims with its enormous mouth open, sea water flows into its mouth. The water filters through its gills. Small fish, shrimp, and plankton (microscopic plants and animals) are caught.

Unlike many sharks. Whale sharks are not a threat to humans. In fact, divers who study them may approach them without fear. Some divers have actually ridden whale sharks. The sharks does not seem to mind.

Revision

3.7 Destruction of Pompeii

Pompeii was a Roman city in ancient Italy. The city was built a few miles south of Mt. Vesuvius. Mt. Vesuvius was an active volcano then. It remains active today. Pompeii was a wealthy city. Pompeii was always busy with commerce and trade.

The day of August 24 in the year A.D. 79, nearly two thousand years ago, began like any other. Without warning. The summit of Vesuvius exploded. Great clouds of smoke and ash were sent high into the sky. Soon the light of the sun was blocked. A terrifying shadow descended over the land.

People awoke that day. They went to work. Began their chores. In the distance Vesuvius sent lazy swirls of dark smoke into the sky, this was normal. No one was worried. The day seemed like any other. There was no cause for worry.

The eruption continued throughout the day and night. Ash bombarded the city. Molten rock bombarded the city. Choking smoke and gas made it impossible to breathe. People panicked. They tried to flee, the streets became jammed, they could not get away in time.

Complete was the destruction of the city. It is estimated that two thousand people died. The doomed city of Pompeii disappeared in a day.

3.8 Trail to the West

Directions: Revise the article and make any changes you feel will improve it. Especially pay attention to sentence structure and active constructions. Rewrite the revised article on a separate sheet of paper.

The Oregon Trail was the most important pioneer route to the American Northwest. The Oregon Trail was about two thousand miles long. Stretching across the plains and through the mountains. Starting in Independence, Missouri. It ended at the Columbia River in Oregon.

The journey over the trail was long by wagon train. It was difficult, too, and dangerous, the trip could take as long as six months. Most wagon trains managed to travel only about fifteen miles per day.

Many hardships were faced by the pioneers. They had to survive terrible storms, the threat of starvation, and possible attacks by Native Americans. Disease could strike suddenly. It could kill entire families. Sometimes as many as half or more of the people of a wagon train died before reaching Oregon.

Despite the hardships and the heartache. The trail was traveled by thousands of pioneers. They believed that by following the Oregon Trail they would be led to a new life.

Revision

3.9 J. K. Rowling and Harry Potter

Joanne Kathleen Rowling was born on July 31, 1965, near Bristol, England. She is known throughout the world as the author of the Harry Potter books.

The idea of writing a fantasy about a young wizard, Harry Potter, was thought of by Rowling in 1990. While she was riding a train. For the next several years the first book of the series was worked on by Rowling.

When she finished the book, Rowling sent it to publishers. The book was turned down by several. Eventually, in 1998, *Harry Potter and the Sorcerer's Stone* was published in the United States. The fantasy focuses on Harry Potter. He is a lonely orphan. He learns that he is a wizard. When Harry enrolls in Hogwarts School of Witchcraft and Wizardry. The magical adventure begins.

The Harry Potter books have proven to be immensely popular, hundreds of millions of the books have been sold. The books have been translated into more than sixty languages and can be bought in two hundred countries, movie versions of the books have been equally popular. Fans around the world continue to be enchanted by the magic of Harry Potter.

3.10 New House

Vanessa was in her new room in her family's new house. Boxes are everywhere. In some places they were on top of each other right up to the ceiling. The room was enormous, much bigger than her room in the old house. Her old room was little compared to this room. But the new room did not feel like home.

Vanessa sighed. She missed her old house. She misses her old friends. She is worried about making new friends.

After she unpacks a few boxes, Vanessa went downstairs and went outside. She sits on the front steps. She looked around the big yard. There was a rose garden, flower beds, and trees. Vanessa had to admit that the yard was pretty. But she doubted she would ever feel at home here.

A little while later, Vanessa noticed a girl at the house across the street. The girl started coming toward her. The girl is about her own age.

"Hi, I'm Rebecca," the girl says. She had a friendly smile. "But my friends call me Becky. . . ."

Revision

3.11 Room Disaster

Marcus was in his room. He could not find his history report. He looked around the room. He thought of how messy it was. No, he decided. It was more than messy. It was a disaster.

He tried to remember where he had put the report. He had finished it yesterday. He finished it after school. Then he had played games online with his friends.

He looked at his desk. So much stuff was on it that he could hardly see the top. He searched through the things on it. He searched the drawers. He searched through the things that lay on his dresser. He searched under his bed. All he found there were old sneakers.

Where was the report? He was desperate. Suddenly he remembered.

He picked up his knapsack. He had put the report in the knapsack yesterday so that he would not lose it. He looked inside. There it was.

Marcus heard the school bus. The driver honked the horn. Marcus grabbed his knapsack. He went to the door. The school bus was driving away.

3.12 The Rocket

Directions: Revise the story and make any changes you feel will improve it. Especially pay attention to strong verbs and verb tenses. Rewrite the revised story on a separate sheet of paper.

Gabriela was in front of the big roller coaster. Anthony, her younger brother, was with her.

The roller coaster was called the Rocket. It was the biggest and fastest coaster Gabriela had ever seen. She had been looking forward to riding it for weeks. But now she is not sure she wants to. Gabriela likes fast rides, but this one makes her scared.

"Come on, Gabriela," says Anthony. "Let's get in line." He takes her hand and started pulling her toward the line of people waiting to ride the Rocket.

At first Gabriela does not move. It was as if her feet will not go. She looks at the coaster as it goes slowly to the top of the tracks. Reaching the peak, it comes roaring down so fast that Gabriela was certain she felt the ground shake.

"Gabriela, come on," said Anthony. "You're not afraid, are you?"

Gabriela gave him a smile. If her little brother was not afraid, she should not be afraid either. She takes a deep breath.

"Let's go," Gabriela says. She led Anthony to the line.

3.13 Pressure Shot

Directions: Revise the story and make any changes you feel will improve it. Especially pay attention to point of view, strong verbs, and distinct descriptions. Rewrite the revised story on a separate sheet of paper.

Ten seconds were left in the championship soccer game between the Lions and the Falcons. The score was tied 2 to 2.

Kara Johnson, the Lions' youngest player, was dribbling the ball upfield toward the Falcons' goal. Her heart was going fast. She was tense. Kara was only in the game because Sharon Wilson, the Lions' best scorer, had been hurt earlier.

As Kara went by a Falcon defender, she saw a small opening toward the right side of the field. I tried to keep all of my attention focused on the ball. I knew I would have only one chance for a shot.

She went by another defender and kept moving.

"Take the shot, Kara!" I heard Sharon's voice from the sideline above the noise of the crowd.

Kara looked at the goal. The goalie was in position, staring at me. I knew I could not shoot the ball past her like this.

Kara tried to trick the goalie into thinking she was about to try a shot. She moved to her left to gain a better angle. She kicked the ball as hard as she could.

The goalie could not stop the ball, and I watched the ball go into the goal.

3.14 Stars

On a clear night a person can see a few thousand stars. You must be away from the lights of cities and towns to see this many stars. This is only a tiny part of a universe that contains billions of galaxies. Each galaxy contain billions of stars. Stars are giant balls of burning gases. They are made up mostly of hydrogen. This is a gas. Inside a star enormous pressure results in nuclear fusion. During fusion, hydrogen atoms are fused. Or forced together, to make helium. During fusion great amounts of energy is produced. The heat and light of a star are created by fusion. The closest star to the Earth is the sun. Without the light and heat of the sun, the Earth would be a cold, dark, lifeless planet. In recent years, it has been discovered by astronomers that numerous stars have planets orbiting them. Our solar system no longer appears to be unique. In fact, it may be quite ordinary. Although we do not yet have the technological capability to travel to distant stars. Maybe someday we will. How wondrous it will be to find Earth-like planets in orbit around other stars. Future generations of human beings would in time makes their homes throughout the stars.

Revision

3.15 About Bears

Directions: Revise the article and make any changes you feel will improve it. Rewrite the revised article on a separate sheet of paper.

Bears are large mammals. They have heavy bodies, short tails, and rounded ears. Although they are classified as carnivores. Most bears also eat grasses, herbs, berries, nuts, and honey. Carnivores are meat-eaters. There are several kinds of bears. North American black bears, grizzly bears, and polar bears are among the most well known. North American black bears are native to North America. This is as their name implies. Black bears are one of the smallest bears. They weigh between two hundred and four hundred pounds. Grizzly bears are much larger than black bears. They can weigh up to a thousand pounds. Grizzlies may be brown, black, or cream-colored. The fur on their shoulders and backs are often tipped with white. This gives them a "grizzled" look. Polar bears are some of the biggest bears. They may be ten feet tall and weigh up to fifteen hundred pounds. They live on the islands of the Arctic Ocean. Seals, young walruses, and fish are hunted by polar bears. In the past, bears are found throughout much of the world. Today they are found mostly in wilderness areas.

3.16 New Madrid, Missouri, Earthquake

Directions: Revise the article and make any changes you feel will improve it. Rewrite the revised article on a separate sheet of paper.

On December 16, 1811, the residents of New Madrid, Missouri, were awakened by a powerful earthquake. This was the first of three great earthquakes. And thousands of lesser aftershocks that struck the region during the winter of 1811–1812.

Many scientists are convinced that the New Madrid earthquakes were among the most powerful ever experienced in North America. If such quakes occurred today in the region. The destruction would be unimaginable. The quakes were so strong that tremors were felt from Canada to Mexico and from the Rocky Mountains to the East Coast. So strong were the quakes that several towns in the region were destroyed, islands in the Mississippi River disappeared, and new lakes were formed. Eyewitness accounts of survivors reported wide cracks opening in the ground, the ground rolling in waves, and large sections of land rising and sinking, damage from the quakes was reported as far away as Charleston, South Carolina, and Washington, DC.

When the next great earthquake will strike the region cannot be predicted by scientists. Many worry that another major quake is only a matter of time.

Revision

3.17 Dr. Daniel Hale Williams

Directions: Revise the article and make any changes you feel will improve it. Rewrite the revised article on a separate sheet of paper.

Daniel Hale Williams (1858–1931) is an African-American physician. He performed the first successful heart surgery. This happened in 1893.

On July 9th of that year, James Cornish, a young man, was stabbed in the chest. He was brought to Provident Hospital. Williams was a surgeon there. Cornish has lost much blood. He needed surgery to stop the bleeding. In those days internal operations almost always result in death from infection. Williams knew that. Without surgery Cornish would surely die. Williams decided to operate.

During surgery, Williams found that Cornish's pericardium had been wounded. The pericardium is a sac of tissue that surrounds the heart. Williams washed the wound with a salt solution. He was hoping this would reduce the chance for infection. He stitched the wound, then he completed the operation. James Cornish survived. He lived for many more years afterward.

Williams goes on to become one of the most respected surgeons of his day. He became, in 1913, the first African-American to be inducted into the American College of Surgeons.

3.18 Ice Skater

Directions: Revise the story and make any changes you feel will improve it. Rewrite the revised story on a separate sheet of paper.

With incredibly and extremely nervous fingers Caitlyn laced her ice skates. She took a deep breath. Hoping to steady the uneasiness in her stomach.

"Don't worry," her coach said. "This time you'll do it."

That only made Caitlyn worry more. Caitlyn recalled her first attempt at completing an axel. A jump with one and a half turns in the air. She had jumped. But had fallen on her landing. The sharp, knifing pain of her breaking ankle would forever be remembered by Caitlyn. Months passed before her ankle was fully healed.

It was only a few weeks ago that Caitlyn had started skating again. She had not attempted an axel, she would today.

Caitlyn stood, stepped onto the ice, and began skating, her heart was thumping.

"You can do it," she was told by her coach.

Caitlyn nodded, forced a weak smile.

She skated around the rink. Trying to build up her courage.

Gaining speed, she knew it was now or never. She pushed off the ice and propelled herself into the air. She spun.

Her landing was good enough to be perfect.

Revision

3.19 Arctic Tern

Arctic terns are small seabirds. They are champion travelers. They make the longest migration of any bird.

Each year Arctic terns fly from the Arctic to Antarctica. Then they fly back to the Arctic. The total distance is nearly twenty-two thousand miles. This is approximately the circumference of the Earth. You have probably learned about circumference in your math class, when studying geometry.

The terns spend the northern summers in the Arctic tundra. They breed there and make their nests. The northern winter approaches, the terns begin flying southward. They finally reach the edge of the Antarctic ice pack. The seasons of the northern and southern hemispheres are reversed. It is now summer in Antarctica. Once summer in Antarctica ends, the terns begin flying northward again. They return to the Arctic.

Arctic terns are only twelve to fifteen inches long and weigh less than a pound. They are well adapted for their long journeys. They have strong wings and streamlined bodies. They eat small fish, shrimp, and krill. Terns swoop down into the water to catch their prey.

Arctic terns have a life span of about twenty years, they spend much of their lives flying.

3.20 Ancient Olympics

The ancient Olympic Games were played in Greece. They were played in the wooded valley of Olympia. The ancient games were held for over a thousand years. They were held every four years. They were begun in 776 B.C. and continued until A.D. 393. This is a long time by anyone's standards.

No one knows who organized the first games. According to myth, Hercules started the games. Hercules was a legendary hero known throughout Greece. The poet Pindar, in a poem he wrote in the fifth century B.C., claims a warrior named Pelops created the games. This was in celebration of a great victory.

The first Olympics were rather small. Only one event was held. This was the stade. It was a footrace of about two hundred yards. In time, a forty-thousand-seat stadium was built, more races were added, as well as wrestling, chariot racing, and the pentathlon were added. The pentathlon was a five-part event that included running, wrestling, jumping, and throwing the discus and javelin. People from all over Greece came to watch the games.

The Olympics were enormously popular. In times of war, truces were called. This allowed athletes and spectators to travel to Olympia safely. It is upon this grand tradition that the modern Olympic Games are founded.

Revision

3.21 Dinosaurs and Birds

When you see a bird. You are looking at a descendant of a dinosaur. Many scientists are now convinced that birds are directly related to the dinosaurs. That walked the Earth millions of years ago.

The evidence for the dinosaur–bird link is strong. Just like modern birds, many dinosaurs walked on their hind legs. They had three forward-pointing toes. They also had long tails. In the 1990s, paleontologists found fossils of dinosaurs in northeastern China. Many of these fossils all had evidence of feathers. Not long after this time, more fossilized skeletons of dinosaurs were found. They showed evidence of feathers and other birdlike features.

The best evidence came in 2000. The fossil of a small dinosaur was found by paleontologists. They named this dinosaur *Microraptor zhaoianus*. It was about the size of a crow. This fossil closely resembled a bird.

Despite the evidence of birdlike features. Most scientists do not consider these dinosaurs to be true birds. At least not what we think of as being birds. It is much, much more likely these creatures are a link between dinosaurs and birds.

The dinosaurs are extinct. Their descendants are alive and well.

© Gary Robert Muschla

Revision

3.22 The Maya

Directions: Revise the article and make any changes you feel will improve it. Rewrite the revised article on a separate sheet of paper.

The Maya were among the most advanced native civilizations of the Americas. Starting around 2600 B.C. They slowly gained power and influence. The Maya came to control much land. Today much of this land is now southern Mexico, Guatemala, Belize, and Honduras.

From about A.D. 200 through 900, their society was among the most advanced in the world. The Maya constructed great cities. They constructed magnificent buildings. They constructed pyramids that served as temples. They developed hieroglyphic writing. They developed an accurate calendar. Mayan astronomers recorded the movements of the sun, planets, and stars.

Around 900, the Maya started to decline. No one knows why. Some historians believe the decline might have been caused by several factors. Including wars, disease, and crop failures over a period of years. This much is known. Cities in southern areas were abandoned. The cities of the north were overcome by an invading group known as the Toltecs.

The Spanish arrived in the sixteenth century. Only a few Mayan cities remained. The great civilization was gone.

Revision

3.23 Never Enough Time

Directions: Revise the story and make any changes you feel will improve it. Rewrite the revised story on a separate sheet of paper.

On Saturday morning Darien woke up very early, much earlier than he usually did. He had so very much to do.

After a quick breakfast of cereal, milk, and juice, Darien rode his bike to soccer practice. He was the goalie for his team, he liked soccer, he had been playing soccer since first grade. He likes to play other sports too.

After lunch, Darien helped his father with work around the house. They planted five new shrubs on the side of the house. His father then waters the shrubs. At the same time, Darien weeds the flower beds. They finished the yard work. They cleaned the garage. This took the rest of the afternoon.

After dinner, Darien's friends came over. His friends were Peter and Ricky. The boys decided to play video games. They play several games. The evening passed quickly, very quickly.

By the time his friends went home, Darien was exhausted. He went to bed. Darien thought of all the things he had to do tomorrow.

Revision

3.24 Kangaroo

Kangaroos are found in Australia and on nearby islands. Most people are not aware that there are about a hundred different species, or kinds, of kangaroos. These range from the tiny kangaroo rat to the giant kangaroo.

The giant kangaroo is one of the best-known species of kangaroo. It is also called the great gray kangaroo. Giant kangaroos stand about five feet tall. They weigh up to 150 pounds. They have a tail of about four feet long. They have sheeplike heads, big ears, short front legs, and large, powerful, exceedingly strong hind legs. With its powerful legs, a giant kangaroo can jump thirty feet in a single hop. It can reach speeds of up to forty miles per hour.

Kangaroos are marsupials. Female marsupials carry their young in pouches. A female kangaroo carries her young in her pouch. A young kangaroo is called a joey. The mother carries the joey in her pouch until it is old enough to survive on its own.

Kangaroos are timid creatures. When attacked, they can be dangerous. They will use their forepaws to "punch" an attacker. They will also use their hind legs to kick and slash. A large kangaroo can seriously injure a person.

Revision

3.25 Myth of Phaeton

Directions: Revise the story and make any changes you feel will improve it. Rewrite the revised story on a separate sheet of paper.

In ancient Greek mythology, Phaeton was the son of Apollo. He was the god of the sun. One day Phaeton went to his father's beautiful and magnificent palace of the sun. Apollo is so pleased to see his son that he promises to grant Phaeton anything he asked.

Phaeton had one desire. He wants to drive Apollo's chariot of the sun across the sky.

Apollo knew this could not be. He warned his son. That no one else—not even the other gods—could drive the chariot of the sun.

Phaeton would not be swayed from his demand. Apollo reluctantly agrees.

Phaeton climbed into the chariot. He whipped the horses. The mighty animals gallop into the sky. They pull the bright sun behind the chariot. But Phaeton quickly lost control of them. They ran low to the Earth. The blazing, hot sun burned the ground and all on it.

Zeus, king of the gods, realized Earth was being destroyed. He hurls a lightning bolt at Phaeton. The boy was killed. The Earth was saved.

From that day on, all understood. Only Apollo could drive the sun's chariot across the sky. And they knew that a person should not try to seize control of natural forces.

Revision

Proofreading

Proofreading is the part of the writing process that puts the final polish on a piece. Proofreading should not be done until writing has been revised. It is a time for you to catch and correct any remaining errors in punctuation, capitalization, spelling, and word usage.

Some students mistakenly believe that proofreading is the easiest of the stages of the writing process. Because revision has been completed, they feel that the writing is done and that proofreading is nothing more than a final glance through the piece to catch any obvious remaining oversights.

Proofreading, however, is just as demanding as the other stages of writing. While it is true that most errors have been corrected by this time, the errors that remain often are hard to find. By now the author may have become so close to the piece that mistakes at this point are not apparent. Moreover, the author is anxious to finish the piece, and he may proofread quickly without the necessary concentration. If an author has done a thorough job of revision, proofreading is much like looking for that needle in a haystack.

For just about every piece, no matter how careful the writer was during revision, a few mistakes remain. Proofreading requires concentration and a good eye.

Proofreading Strategies

Proofreading is different from ordinary reading, which includes a significant amount of skimming. For most material, the average reader focuses on only a few words per line and skims the rest. This is usually enough for the reader to gain an understanding of the material. Proofreading, though, requires that the proofreader read and examine every word and punctuation mark.

When done properly, proofreading is slow, tedious work. Anything less is likely to be inadequate.

Proofreading is the last step before sharing writing with readers. Here are general guidelines for proofreading:

1. Read slowly and concentrate on punctuation, capitalization, spelling, and word usage.
2. Look at the page to make sure paragraphs are fully indented, margins are correct, and there are no gaps in spacing.
3. Proofread the piece two or three times. It is likely that each time a few more minor errors will be found. Only when no more errors are found is proofreading done.

Choose an example of your work to proofread. This might be a previously completed piece, or a piece that you have just finished. Proofread the piece with care and concentration.

Follow the above suggestions whenever proofreading your work. With practice and experience, you will eventually develops your own methods for proofreading.

Proofreading and Computer Screens

Without doubt, computers have made the work of most writers easier. The capabilities of the machines for composing and revising are without question. But proofreading on a computer screen can pose problems for writers.

Reading text on a computer screen can be trying to the eyes. Some writers read material less carefully than they do text printed on paper. In addition, text on paper has a different "look" than text on a screen. When an author reads text on paper, he is more likely to concentrate and examine words and punctuation with greater care.

Of course, some writers do quite well proofing on a computer screen. You may eventually fall into this category. Growing up with computers will help you be comfortable writing, revising, and proofreading written material on a screen.

Following are guidelines for proofreading on a computer screen:

1. Read slowly and carefully. [Most people tend to read faster on a computer screen than a printed page.]
2. Use the cursor to go through text one line at a time.
3. Read every word of each line before going to the next line.
4. Concentrate on every piece of punctuation.

5. Use the print preview to check the page for paragraphs, skipped spaces, and unnecessary returns.

Proofread a finished piece on a computer screen for practice. If you are not comfortable proofing on a computer screen, print the material and proof the printed text.

Grammar and Spelling Checkers

Just about all word-processing software includes grammar and spelling checkers. Use these helpful programs, but keep in mind that there are limitations to such programs. Grammar checkers may flag sentence structure that is correct but slightly unconventional. Spelling checkers will flag any word that is not in their dictionary. In some cases, a spelling checker will offer alternatives for correction that are not the word you had in mind. In the cases of both grammar and spelling checkers, you must recognize what is right and what is wrong. When in doubt, consult a grammar book or dictionary, both of which you should always have nearby during proofreading.

Proofreading Partners

Because writers often have trouble stepping back from their writing to view their work objectively, proofreading can be difficult. The author may pass over minor errors that others quickly recognize. A proofreading partner can help find many of the errors that the writer may overlook.

Proofreading partners can help each other become better writers. During proofreading students should underline any errors they find in their partner's work. An alternative to marking clean pages is to use stick-on notes. If you and your partner cannot agree whether an item is wrong, you should consult a dictionary or grammar book.

Exercise 4.3 Partners for Proofing

Work with a partner or friend. You are to proofread each other's writing and identify any remaining errors in punctuation, capitalization, spelling, or word usage. Underline any mistakes you find, or use stick-on notes. After proofreading, the proofreader consults with the author and notes the mistakes she found. If the author disagrees with any of the supposed mistakes, you should check a reference source. The author then corrects any mistakes and proceeds to produce the final copy. Proofread the piece once more and correct any mistakes that may have managed to slip through the previous proofreadings. Then switch roles; the previous author becomes the proofreader for her partner's work and the previous proofreader assumes the role of author.

Proofreading is not a task of writing to be taken lightly. It is the final preparation of a piece for its audience.

Worksheets

Proofreading is a challenging task. The worksheets in this section are designed to provide you with practice in proofreading.

The worksheets, which include both articles and stories, cover a variety of topics. Errors are concentrated in punctuation, capitalization, and word usage. The "Guidelines for Proofreading" on page 185 offer direction for your proofreading efforts.

The worksheets proceed from relatively basic—for example, focusing on end punctuation, commas, and capitalization—to more challenging. Along with general errors in punctuation and capitalization, the directions for Worksheets 4.1 through 4.15 focus on specific errors. Worksheets 4.16 through 4.25 do not provide any hints of what to look for. The worksheets average about ten errors each, some a few less and some a few more. Many of the errors are obvious; some are tricky and require sharp concentration.

The Answer Key for the worksheets begins on page 211. While most of the corrections are clear-cut, a few, especially concerning the use of commas, are open to interpretation of the context.

As you gain experience with proofreading, your proofreading skills will grow. Proofreading will help you to present polished writing to your readers.

Guidelines for Proofreading

Use the following guidelines when proofreading your writing.

1. Sentences begin with capital letters.

2. Sentences end with correct punctuation.

3. Paragraphs are indented.

4. Proper nouns and proper adjectives are capitalized.

5. Commas are used correctly (between the items in a list, to connect compound sentences, and after introductory words, phrases, and clauses).

6. Apostrophes are used correctly (with possessive nouns and contractions).

7. Pronouns are used correctly.

8. Quotation marks are used correctly (for dialogue, and for the titles of short stories, articles, poems, and songs).

9. Italics and underlining are used correctly (for the titles of books, the names of newspapers and magazines, and the titles of CDs, television shows, and movies).

10. Words are used correctly (especially homophones such as *there*, *their*, and *they're*; *your* and *you're*; *its* and *it's*; *whose* and *who's*; *hear* and *here*; *for* and *four*; *buy*, *by*, and *bye*; and *to*, *too*, and *two*).

Proofreading

4.1 Lightning and Thunder

Directions: Proofread and correct the article. Pay close attention to errors in ending punctuation, commas, and capitalization. Make your corrections on this sheet.

If you have ever been caught in a thunderstorm you may have been frightened by the lightning and thunder. Have you ever wondered what causes lightning and thunder.

The air within a thunderstorm is turbulent. As warm air rises and cool air falls water droplets, and ice crystals crash into each other. These collisions cause electrical charges to build up. Positive charges collect in the upper parts of the clouds, and negative charges collect in the lower parts. To balance the negative charges, positive charges also collect near the ground. As this process continues the charges increase in strength. Because unlike charges attract, Electricity may jump from one cloud to another, or between a cloud and the ground. We see this, as lightning.

A lightning bolt is extremely hot. It heats air Molecules and causes them to expand violently This causes a powerful vibration that we hear as thunder.

Thunder can be loud and frightening, but lightning is dangerous. when a thunderstorm approaches you should seek shelter indoors. Stay away from windows, and doors, and do not use electrical equipment. If you are outside, never stand near a tree? Trees can attract lightning. A lightning strike can be fatal.

Proofreading

4.2 Study Tips for Tests

Directions: Proofread and correct the article. Pay close attention to errors in ending punctuation, commas, and capitalization. Make your corrections on this sheet.

Many students do not know how to study for tests. Are you one of them. If you think you are, the following tips can help.

Preparation for any test, begins long before the day of the test. Keep up with your daily work and take accurate notes On the days leading up to the test, listen to any reviews your teacher gives. This will help you to identify what may be on the test. This in turn, will help you to study the right material. If you have any questions about any of the material, ask your Teacher?

A day, or two before the test, you should go over your notes and key parts of your textbook. Do not wait until the last minute to study. students who study ahead of time, usually do better than those who cram at the last minute.

Get a good night's sleep before the test wake up on time, and eat a solid breakfast. Take the test with confidence. If you have studied effectively you are likely to do well.

Proofreading

4.3 Family Gathering

Martina woke up early on thanksgiving morning. Anxious to start the day, she dressed quickly and scampered downstairs

She found her mother in the Kitchen preparing food to take to Martina's grandmother's house. That was where the entire family gathered every thanksgiving for dinner. All of Martina's Uncles Aunts and cousins would be there

After breakfast, Martina helped her mother pack food in a big cooler. They packed, salad, fresh vegetables, fruits, and two cream pies.

Martina's grandmother lived about three hours away, and the drive seemed to take forever. As they drove Martina wondered how many family members had already arrived? When Martina's father pulled into the driveway, she saw several cars.

Martina smiled. Everyone was here. Having Thanksgiving with the family was always, a wonderful time.

4.4 From Tadpole to Frog

Directions: Proofread and correct the article. Pay close attention to errors in ending punctuation, commas, and capitalization. Make your corrections on this sheet.

Frogs are interesting Creatures. They go through metamorphosis, a complete change in structure during their lives They begin life as a fishlike tadpole and grow into a frog.

Tadpoles hatch from eggs. They breathe with gills have streamlined bodies, and have tails. They feed on algae, and tiny Vegetation

As a tadpole matures, its gills disappear lungs develop and legs start to grow. In time the tadpole starts eating insects and larger plant matter.

After about nine weeks of life, the tadpole looks more like a frog with a tail than a tadpole. Eventually the tail is absorbed into the tadpole's body. by about the fourth month of its life, a tadpole has made the transition to a frog. Metamorphosis is finished

The Cycle is now ready to repeat. Female frogs lay their eggs in water, from which a new generation of tadpoles hatches.

Proofreading

4.5 Madam C. J. Walker

Madam C. J. Walker, (1867–1919), was the most successful African-American businesswoman of the early twentieth Century. She became the first African-American woman Millionaire.

Madam Walker, whose birth name was Sarah Breedlove built a company that sold hair products for African-American women. To help the company grow; Madam Walker tirelessly promoted her products. By 1910, her company had become so successful that she was able to put others in charge of the day-to-day operations. This allowed her to devote more time to lecture on issues that affected African americans. In her later years, Madam Walker supported numerous African-American schools charities and organizations

When Madam Walker died, at the age of fifty-one, she was thought to be the wealthiest African-American woman in the United States. Her life was an inspiration to women throughout the Country.

4.6 The Key

Samantha hurried down the empty hallway toward her classroom. School had ended an hour ago and she hoped her classroom was not locked. She needed to get her Science book, which she had forgotten to take home. Without the book, she wouldnt be able to study for the big science test tomorrow.

Science was a difficult subject for Samantha. She had to study more for science than for any other subject.

When she got to her classroom, Samantha was relieved to find the door open. She went inside, expecting to see mrs. Talbot her teacher but the room was empty. Samantha figured that mrs Talbot had gone home for the day.

As Samantha walked by the teachers desk, she noticed a paper on it. Her eyes widened. It was the answer key to the test. The key could help her get a good grade.

Samantha stood there for a long moment. Taking the answers would be cheating and that was wrong.

She went to her desk got her science book, and left the room.

4.7 First Flight

Directions: Proofread and correct the article. Pay close attention to errors in punctuation and capitalization. Especially pay attention to the use of commas and apostrophes. Make your corrections on this sheet.

People have dreamed about flying for thousands of years. Early ideas ranged from mechanical wings that could enable a person to fly like a bird; to strange machines with flapping blades. None, of course worked.

As time passed, people looked for other ways to fly. A breakthrough came in france in 1782.

Joseph and Jacques Montgolfier, two Brothers were interested in flying. While sitting by a fireplace, Joseph filled a paper bag with smoke and hot air. As the Brothers watched the bag float up to the ceiling they got an idea.

The Montgolfier's began to experiment. They made balloons out of paper and linen and filled them with hot air from a fire. When they released the balloons the balloons rose. The brothers built bigger and bigger balloons until they built one able to carry people.

Finally, in November of 1783, two people, flew in a Montgolfier balloon. This first flight lasted twenty-five minutes and covered about five miles. The dream of flight became, a reality.

4.8 Shaking Earth

Earthquakes may best be described as a shaking of the Earth. Thousands of earthquakes occur each year but only one out of five is strong enough to be felt. On average, of every thousand earthquakes only two cause damage

Earthquakes are caused by movement of the Earths crust. The Earth's crust, which is it's outer layer is divided into great pieces. These pieces called plates are made of rock. The plates move slowly in different directions. They may grind past each other away from each other or toward each other. Sometimes a long crack, called a fault, forms between plates. The famous San Andreas fault in california is a result of two plates grinding past each other. If enough stress builds up along a fault an earthquake occurs.

Minor earthquakes cause little damage, and few injuries. Major quakes can destroy entire cities and result in thousands of deaths.

Proofreading

4.9 Track Meet

It was the biggest regional Track Meet of the season. Andrew stretched and tried to shake the nervous tension, from his body. So far this year he had won all of the two-mile races he had entered but now he was facing boys who might be faster and have greater endurance.

The official called the boys to the starting line. Andrew took a deep breath and stepped forward.

"Remember Andrew," Coach Simmons said, "Pace yourself. Make sure you're strong for the end."

Andrew nodded. He took his position on the inside lane. He thought about his coachs advice. Andrew sometimes made the mistake of running too hard in the first part of a race. When he did that he would fade at the end.

"On your mark! said the official. Get set! Go!"

The race began.

Andrew was in the middle of the pack of runners his strides long and easy. It was a long way to the end of the race. He would make sure he was strong for the finish.

4.10 Business Letter

Directions: Proofread and correct the letter. Pay close attention to errors in punctuation and capitalization. Especially pay attention to the use of commas, apostrophes, and colons. Make your corrections on this sheet.

123 River Drive

Green Valley NJ 00000

Oct 25 2010

Ms Janice Williams, Circulation Manager

Extreme Skateboarding Magazine

50 Reynolds street

Mountain Lake, CA 00000

Dear Ms. Williams,

I would like to subscribe to *Extreme Skateboarding Magazine*. Enclosed is a check for $24.95 for a subscription for one year.

Thank you.

Sincerely Yours'.

Thomas Jackson

4.11 Great Friends

Directions: Proofread and correct the article. Pay close attention to errors in punctuation and capitalization. Especially pay attention to the use of apostrophes and pronouns. Make your corrections on this sheet.

Richie and me are best friends. We've been best friends for about as long as I can remember.

Some kids think its strange that a girl and boy in seventh grade are best friends. But I dont think its strange at all. Richie and me have a lot in common.

We've always lived next door to each other. We both like sports we like the same type of music, and we like the same kinds of Movies. But most important, we just like hanging out together. There's never any trouble between Richie and I. We stick up for each other, and we're always honest with each other. Richies easy to talk to and he's always willing to help when I have a problem. I do the same for him.

No matter what happens I know I can depend on Richie, and he knows he can depend on me. I suppose that, most of all is what makes our friendship so special.

Proofreading

4.12 Amelia Earhart

What happened to Amelia Earhart. People have been trying to answer this question since 1937. That was the year Earhart and Fred J. Noonan her copilot disappeared in their plane near Howland island in the South Pacific.

Amelia Earhart loved to fly. She became famous in may of 1932 when she made a solo flight across the Atlantic ocean. She followed this feat with several solo long-distance flights across the U.S. In January of 1931, she made a solo flight from Hawaii to California.

Earhart attempted her most daring flight in June of 1937. With copilot Noonan, she set off to make an around-the-world flight. On July 2nd there plane vanished. Rescue teams mounted extensive search efforts but no sign of Earhart, Noonan, or they're plane was ever found.

In the following years, researchers and mystery buffs have tried to discover what happened to Amelia Earhart. None have succeeded and Amelia Earharts disappearance remains a mystery.

Proofreading

4.13 Season Opener

Giorgio stared at the overcast sky. He turned to Danny his friend.

"It looks like rain" Giorgio said.

"According to the weather forecast, said Danny, "theres only a slight chance of showers."

The two boys had just arrived at the baseball field for the first game of the season. Some of the players of both teams were already their.

Coach Bennett instructed the boys to begin warming up.

Giorgio and Danny took their places with there teammates and began playing catch.

Giorgio looked back at the sky. Baseball was his favorite sport and he had been looking forward to this first game for weeks.

Giorgio quit worrying" said Danny. "the game will start on time."

"I hope so," said Giorgio.

A little while later, the sun poked through the clouds.

"See," said Danny. "The suns coming out. Now you'll be worrying about the sun getting into your eyes."

Giorgio smiled. "Your probably right."

4.14 Reading Enjoyment

Directions: Proofread and correct the article. Pay close attention to errors in punctuation and capitalization. Especially pay attention to the use of quotation marks, italics, and apostrophes. Make your corrections on this sheet.

Step into my house, and you will find books and magazines everywhere. Everybody in my family enjoys reading. We read for entertainment, and information.

My father rides the bus to work each morning. During his commute he reads "The New York Times." He also reads magazines. His favorites are *Time* and *Discover*.

My mother enjoys reading novels. She reads a new novel every week. She likes mysteries the best but she also likes romances. Sometimes she likes a book so much that she cant put it down until she finishes it.

Jessica, my older sister likes short stories and poems. One of her favorite short stories' is *The dinner Party* by Mona Gardner. Her favorite poem is Lewis Carroll's "Jabberwocky."

As for me I mostly read novels. My favorites are fantasies with heroes, evil villains, and magic. If I had to pick one favorite, I would choose "*The Hobbit*" by J. R. R Tolkien.

Proofreading

4.15 Big Slope

Emily stuck her ski poles into the snow to steady herself. She stood on the top of the mountain and looked down the slope. Daredevil trail disappeared in the distance.

She felt a gentle pat on her shoulder.

"You can make it down," said Alyssa her big sister.

"Thats not what worries me, said Emily. She forced a smile. "Im worried about how many broken bones I'll have."

"You don't have too do this, Alyssa said."

"Yes, I do" said Emily, who prided herself on her skill at skiing. "This is the only trail on this mountain I've never gone down."

Alyssa smiled. "You'll be fine," she said. "Keep your knees bent and remember to lean into the turns.

Emily nodded. "Hear I go." She pushed off with her poles and started down the trail.

She heard Alyssas voice behind her.

"You can do it."

As Emily leaned into the first turn she hoped her sister was right.

4.16 Sound Waves

Directions: Proofread and correct the article. Pay close attention to errors in punctuation, capitalization, and word usage. Make your corrections on this sheet.

The sounds of laughter, the honking of a car horn and the roar of a lawn mowers motor are all produced in the same way. But do you know how those sounds are produced.

All sounds are a result of vibrations. When something vibrates it moves back and forth rapidly. Imagine plucking a string on a Violin. As the string vibrates, it makes a sound. Of course you seldom see the vibrations that cause sound, because the vibrations are to small and are moving too fast. Unlike plucking a string, imagine tapping a pencil on a desk. You cant see the vibrations but you hear the sound of the tapping.

When an object vibrates it causes the nearby molecules in the air to move. As the molecules move, the vibrations travel through the air in the form of waves. Like the ripples that result from a stone tossed in a pond, the waves move outward from the point of the sound in every direction. When these waves reach your ear, you here the sound.

As sound waves move outward from a vibrating object, they become weaker. This is why a sound becomes fainter the farther away you are from it's source.

Proofreading

4.17 Chess

Have you ever played chess. If you have you have played a game that has been around for at least fifteen hundred years.

Chess is a game of skill, and strategy played by two players. The game is based on the warfare of the Middle Ages. Each player has sixteen pieces that he plays on a square board. The board is divided into sixty-four alternate light and dark squares. When a player lands a peace on a space occupied by one of his opponents pieces, that piece is removed from the board. The object of the game is to capture, or checkmate, the opponent's king. Capture of the king ends the game.

No one knows whom invented chess? Most historians believe the game originated in india about the sixth century A.D. The game slowly spread westward threw Persia (modern Iran) and reached Europe sometime between 700 and 900.

The modern game began to evolve during the sixteenth and seventeenth Centuries. Today, chess is played around the world and is as popular as ever.

Proofreading

4.18 Volcanoes

A volcano is a mountain with a vent, or opening to the interior of the Earth. Magma (hot, melted rock) from inside the Earth passes through the vent to the surface. Sometimes the magma flows out slowly but sometimes it erupts in great explosions.

Volcanoes can be in one of three states, active, dormant, or extinct. An active volcano is erupting or shows signs of erupting soon. A dormant volcano has not erupted in some time but may erupt again in the future. An extinct volcano is no longer capable of erupting.

Volcanic eruptions start far beneath the surface. When magma comes under great pressure, it rises threw cracks and week spots in the rock. Eventually the magma finds it's way to the surface. If the pressure is intense, the magma may erupt. Along with magma, eruptions usually include gases ash, and steam.

Magma that flows out of a volcano is called Lava. Lava can reach temperatures of 2,000 degrees Fahrenheit or more. Flowing down a volcanos sides lava can destroy everything in its path.

Scientists study volcanoes, in the hope of learning how to predict eruptions. Such knowledge would help them warn people before an eruption occurs.

Proofreading

4.19 Looking for Whales

Directions: Proofread and correct the story. Pay close attention to errors in punctuation, capitalization, and word usage. Make your corrections on this sheet.

Brianna stepped from the dock and into the boat. She plopped onto the nearest seat. She was not happy being here. Her and her parents were about to spend one of there vacation days in search of whales. Brianna would have preferred to spend the day at the oceanside resort where the family was staying for the weak.

"I've been looking forward to today for months Briannas mother said.

"I haven't." Brianna said. "I'd rather be at the beach."

"You can go to the beach every day for the rest of our vacation said her father. "But if we're lucky, today you can see a whale."

Brianna didnt like boats and she liked the idea of searching for whales even less.

As the boat left the dock, Brianna sighed. This was going to be a long day.

It was early afternoon when the Captain directed everyone to look ahead.

"There! cried one of the passengers.

Brianna looked and saw a magnificent animal rise from the water.

"Its incredible," she said, suddenly glad she was hear and not back on the beach.

4.20 Color the World

Directions: Proofread and correct the article. Pay close attention to errors in punctuation, capitalization, and word usage. Make your corrections on this sheet.

One of the most wonderful features of the world is color. Colors help to make things distinct. Just think, of a blue sky, a red rose, or the pure whiteness of freshly fallen snow. Can you imagine how dull the world would be without color.

The basics of colors are surprisingly simple. Colors can be divided into three kinds primary, secondary, and intermediate. The primary colors are red, yellow, and blue. They cant be made bye mixing any other colors. The secondary colors, which are made by mixing to primary colors are orange green, and violet. Mixing red and yellow makes orange. Mixing yellow and blue makes green. Mixing blue and red makes violet. Intermediate colors are made by mixing primary and secondary colors. Mixing white, or black with colors will make them lighter or darker.

Its remarkable that all colors are based on combinations of red, yellow, and blue. The World truly is a colorful place.

Proofreading

4.21 Cat in the Tree

I was upstairs working on my book report when Marlena my little sister called me from downstairs.

"Come quick Angela!" she cried.

"What's wrong," I said, getting up from my desk and hurrying to the stairs.

"Its Puffin! Marlena said. She's in a big tree. She cant get down." Puffin was our cat.

I hurried downstairs and followed Marlena out the front door.

Looking up at the big oak tree in our yard I saw Puffin sitting on a high branch. She had climbed up but she was afraid to climb down.

"Puffin, come down right now," I said. A mournful meow was my answer.

Their wasn't anything I could do except to keep calling Puffin down. But the cat wouldnt budge.

I was glad when my Father came home from work. He got a ladder, climbed up, and got Puffin.

I smiled as Marlena scolded the foolish cat.

"Puffin I never want you to climb that tree again," she said.

4.22 Catching Rainbows

If you have ever seen a rainbow in the sky you have witnessed one of the beauties of nature. The typical rainbow makes an arc in the sky. Sometimes a rainbow is so big that it's ends seem to touch the Earth.

The mystery of a rainbow lies in sunlight and water droplets. A ray of sunlight contains all the colors of the spectrum, red, orange, yellow, green, blue, and violet. When sunlight shines through water droplets the droplets separate the sunlight into its different colors. Under the right conditions this creates a rainbow.

Rainbows may appear anywhere sunlight shines on water droplets: but they most often are seen near the end of a rain shower. They may also appear in the spray of a waterfall a fountain or a garden hose.

According to Legend a pot of gold awaits you at the end of a rainbow. Of course you can never reach the end. As you approach a rainbow, the rainbow seems to retreat and soon disappears.

Proofreading

4.23 Babysitting Wars

Directions: Proofread and correct the story. Pay close attention to errors in punctuation, capitalization, and word usage. Make your corrections on this sheet.

Dawn walked up the steps to the home of Mr. and Mrs Ross and rang the doorbell. This was the first time she was to babysit for Matthew, their son. She hoped Matthew, who was only five years old would behave. Christina, Dawn's best friend babysat for Matthew once, and she vowed never to babysit for him again.

Mrs. Ross opened the door and greeted Dawn with a friendly smile.

Dawn saw Matthew standing in the living room. He was smiling to. He seemed like a nice boy.

After Mrs. Ross gave Dawn instructions, her and her husband got ready to leave.

"Remember Dawn," mrs. Ross said at the door, Matthew must be in bed no later than nine oclock."

"I'll remember." Dawn said.

For the next two hours Dawn read to Matthew, they drew and colored, and they watched Matthews favorite video. Matthew was so pleasant that Dawn began to wonder if Christina had babysat for the same boy.

At nine oclock Dawn told Matthew that it was time for bed.

Matthew looked at her and smiled.

"No!" he said firmly. "And you can't make me go to bed.

Dawn thought of Christina and realized that it was going to be a long night.

4.24 Wrestling Challenge

> **Directions:** Proofread and correct the story. Pay close attention to errors in punctuation, capitalization, and word usage. Make your corrections on this sheet.

It was the final day of wrestling camp. Dan was to wrestle Brett in the championship match for there weight class.

Dan looked at Brett and frowned. He doubted that he could defeat Brett. Brett was a year older and had more experience.

"Bretts a great wrestler," Dan said to Roberto his best friend.

"He is," said Roberto, "But he loses his cool. He likes to pin his opponent's fast. But when that doesn't happen, he gets mad and makes mistakes."

"But how does that help me," said Dan. "He's faster and stronger than I am."

"You have to wrestle smart, said Roberto. "Dont let him gain the advantage. He'll get frustrated and than you make your move."

"You mean stay on defense until he makes a mistake," said Dan.

Roberto nodded.

Soon after the match began, Dan realized his friend was right. When the match was finished Dan was a wrestling champion.

Proofreading

4.25 Deep Space Explorers

Commander Sarto stood on the bridge of his starship and watched the main viewing screen. As they approached the tiny planet it grew on the screen. Sarto studied the oceans and land masses that appeared through the clouds. The planet reminded him of home.

"Take us into orbit," he said to Jartan his second in command. "Then see if you can listen to they're communications."

Sarto thought of his mission to make contact with the Beings that lived on the planet. He wondered what they were like?

He noticed the concern that had come to Jartans face.

"Whats the matter." Sarto said.

"There must be some mistake," said Jartan. "The transmissions I'm picking up indicate that these beings are quite violent." "Their not ready to join the United Planets."

Sarto sighed. He had seen this happen before.

"Sometimes the first survey teams make errors in there evaluations," Sarto said. "Set course for the next planet. Make a note to visit Earth again in about a hundred years."

Answer Key

Part 1

Answers for the worksheets throughout this section will vary, depending on your responses.

Part 2

2.1 Sentences will vary.

2.2 Sentences will vary.

2.3 Sentences may vary. Possible sentences follow. 1. Carl mowed the lawn and trimmed the hedges. 2. It rained all day, and the soccer game was postponed. 3. Maria and Melinda are twins, but they don't look much like each other. 4. The evening grew darker, and the stars soon appeared. 5. Mandy plays soccer and softball. 6. We might go to a movie, or we might go shopping instead. 7. Juan had to do his history report, but he had to finish his math homework first. 8. The kitten crept up and pounced on the toy mouse.

2.4 Sentences may vary. Possible sentences follow. 2. After LuAnn finished her science assignment, she started her math. 3. Because it snowed heavily all night, the roads were impassable. 4. When the power went off last night, Rob realized he did not have a flashlight. 5. Even though Carla had a sprained ankle, she still went to soccer practice. 6. Once the sky became overcast, the rain began. 7. While Trish was home with a cold, she finished reading *Dicey's Song*. 8. During the middle of the night, strange sounds woke Regina.

2.5 If you sometimes wonder what the difference is between a meteoroid, meteor, and meteorite, you are not alone. Many people find these words confusing. ⌐Meteoroids are rocky chunks of matter that hurtle through space. While many are the size of a small stone, others may be hundreds of feet wide. Most meteoroids orbit the sun and never approach Earth. Some, however, have orbits that intersect the orbit of the Earth. If these meteoroids come too close, they may be captured by the Earth's gravity and pulled into the Earth's atmosphere. Friction with the molecules in the atmosphere will cause the meteoroid to heat up and disintegrate. ⌐When a meteoroid begins to burn in the atmosphere, it leaves a streak of light. It is now called a meteor, often mistakenly referred to as a shooting star. Although most meteors disintegrate completely before they hit the ground, some make it through the atmosphere and smash into the Earth. ⌐ A meteor that hits the Earth is called a meteorite. If a meteor is big, the impact will result in a great explosion and terrible destruction. ⌐Fortunately, most meteoroids remain far from the Earth. Of those that enter the atmosphere, most disintegrate long before reaching the ground.

2.6 Topic sentences will vary. Possible sentences follow. 1. Leon had a lot of homework. 2. Jon enjoys playing video games. 3. Jenna is very talented. 4. Christy could not find her book report.

2.7 Transitional sentences will vary. Possible sentences follow. 1. She got to the bus stop as the bus was pulling up. 2. Just as he reached his yard, the rain began to pour down. 3. Curious, she took the CD out. 4. Rolling up his sleeves, he got started.

2.8 Details will vary. Possible details follow. 1. Thunder could be heard in the distance. Trees bent in the gusty winds. People were hurrying inside. 2. She put icing on the cake. She finished putting up the final decorations. She made the punch and filled the punch bowl. 3. She read to the twins. They colored. They watched the twins' favorite TV programs. 4. The land was hot and dry. Flowers withered. The grass was brown.

2.9 Sentences will vary. Possible sentences follow. 2. The rain pounded on the roof and ran down the gutters. 3. When rain ruined our picnic, Aunt Loretta smiled and explained how we would have our picnic indoors. 4. Christina looked at her report card and smiled at all the As. 5. The heavy rain caused the rushing river to rise and wash over its banks. 6. Lisa's heart pounded when she heard the noises outside the front door. 7. Martin dribbled past two defenders and shot the ball perfectly through the basket. 8. The storm knocked over trees and damaged the roofs of several houses.

2.10 Some answers may vary. Possible answers follow. 1. piercing (or frightening) 2. deep, invincible 3. blank (or empty) 4. old, frightening (or strange) 5. mighty (or towering) 6. playful (or fluffy), fluffy (or old) 7. outdoor (or physical or exciting) 8. towering (or mighty), cloudless 9. wintry 10. blazing

2.11 Some answers may vary. Possible answers follow. 1. thoroughly (or carefully) 2. always 3. recently (or easily or quickly) 4. intensely 5. completely 6. flawlessly 7. soon 8. quickly 9. easily 10. carefully (or thoroughly)

2.12 Answers will vary.

2.13 1. Kim was nervous and could not stop fidgeting. This was her first gymnastics competition, and she was afraid she would make mistakes and let her team down. When Carrie, her friend, tried to assure her that she would do fine, Kim smiled. But she still felt nervous. When her coach called her name, Kim stepped forward. She took a deep breath to steady herself and assumed her starting position on the floor.

2. Michael woke up early on Saturday. He knew it was going to be an extremely busy day. That morning, he helped his father mow the lawn and trim the hedges. Right after lunch Michael went to soccer practice. He got home from practice around 4:00 P.M. He watched his younger brother until dinner because his parents had not yet returned from shopping. After dinner Michael did research for his history project. By the time Michael went to sleep that night, he was exhausted.

2.14 2. The wind uprooted the great oak tree. 3. Megan designed the art club's new logo. 4. Trish won the debate. 5. Tony washed the car. 6. Marissa played a violin solo in the eighth-grade winter concert. 7. The fox crept up on the unsuspecting rabbit. 8. The intense snowstorm caused treacherous whiteout conditions. 9. Paula Fox wrote *The Slave Dancer*. 10. Mrs. Carter assigned homework for the spring break.

2.15 Sentences may vary. Possible sentences follow. 2. The hawk soared high over the field in search of prey. 3. The cat crept toward the bird. 4. The girls whispered in the library. 5. Joanna jumped out of the way of the speeding car. 6. The little boy shrieked when he stubbed his toe. 7. Thomas rushed to catch the bus before it pulled away. 8. Alvaro raced to the finish line. 9. The cold winter wind whipped across the open field. 10. The fog blanketed the valley.

2.16 1. present 2. future perfect 3. present 4. past 5. present perfect 6. future 7. past 8. past perfect 9. future 10. present

2.17 1. bakes 2. uses 3. watch 4. jog 5. lives 6. plays 7. helps 8. practice 9. twinkle 10. rises

2.18 I sighed, thinking of all the math and science homework I had to do. I also had to read another chapter in my novel.

I looked at the pile of books on my desk and frowned. I couldn't decide which book to open first, but I knew I had better start if I wanted to meet my friends later.

I opened my math book and began. After I finished ten word problems, I answered my science questions. Finally I read the chapter in my novel.

As soon as I was done, I went to see my friends, who were waiting for me at the basketball court. By the time I arrived, they had already chosen teams. They had saved a spot for me.

2.19 You may select other names for the third person point of view.

Teresa woke up early on the Saturday of the five-kilometer race. Her father and she would be running to help raise money for charity. She had been jogging with him four times a week for the last several weeks, and she was certain she would finish the race.

Once the race began, though, she wasn't so sure. There were a lot of hills, and they were running into the wind. Teresa began to worry that she would become tired and have to walk to the finish line.

Remembering her father's advice about keeping a slow but steady pace, she kept going. When at last she saw the finish line, she smiled and sprinted the last hundred yards.

Teresa didn't win any trophy. But that was OK. She was satisfied simply having run and finished her first big race.

2.20 **Compare:** Both elephants have trunks and eat grass and leaves. **Contrast:** African elephants are found mostly in the tropical forests and grasslands of Africa. They are bigger than Indian elephants and can reach a height of thirteen feet. African elephants are tallest at the shoulder, they have larger ears, and their skin is more wrinkled. Both male and female African elephants have tusks. Indian elephants are found in India and Southeast Asia. Indian elephants are tallest at the arch of the back. Only male Indian elephants have tusks.

2.21 Sentences will vary.

2.22 1. a passageway or opening 2. knowledge, enlightenment 3. obstacle, hindrance 4. sadness, worry, concern 5. a beginning 6. wisdom 7. a journey 8. infinity, endlessness 9. end, finish 10. slyness

Part 3

Revised articles and stories will vary. Possible revisions are provided.

3.1 A hot spring is water that flows out of the ground at temperatures higher than the air temperature. Most hot springs result from underground water flowing over molten or hot rock.

Sometimes the molten rock can heat the water to such high temperatures that the water turns to steam. If the pressure increases enough, steam and water are pushed toward the surface with great force. The steam and water may spout high into the air. This eruption of steam and water is called a geyser.

Most geysers are found in three parts of the world: the western United States, Iceland, and New Zealand. The most famous geyser in the world is Old Faithful in Yellowstone National Park. Most geysers erupt at irregular intervals, but Old Faithful erupts on average once every ninety-four minutes each day. Several thousand gallons of hot water shoot up to 170 feet in the air.

Watching a geyser erupt is a thrilling experience. Geysers are one of nature's most exciting spectacles.

3.2 Comets may be thought of as being big, dirty snowballs in space. Scientists believe that most comets are made up of about 75 percent ice and 25 percent dust and rock.

When a comet approaches the sun, the heat from the sun causes some of the ice to vaporize and glow. As the comet nears the sun, radiation, called the solar wind, sweeps the vaporizing gases away from the comet. This produces a tail. Because of the solar wind, the tail of a comet always streaks away from the sun.

No one knows for certain how comets originated. But many scientists believe comets are leftover matter from the time our solar system formed. They do not know how many comets are in our solar system.

While most comets remain far from Earth, some have hit our planet. A comet impact is thought to have caused a great explosion in Siberia in 1908. Fortunately, comet impacts are rare.

In the past, people looked at comets as evil omens. They thought that comets brought wars, plagues, and death. Today people look at comets with interest and curiosity. They know that comets are simply dirty snowballs in our solar system.

3.3 The origin of the modern roller coaster can be traced to Russian ice slides of the seventeenth century. The slides were first built in the mid-1600s in the area around present-day St. Petersburg.

The ice slides were large wooden structures, some being between seventy and eighty feet high. The slides were covered with ice several inches thick. Large sleds sped down a steep drop that extended hundreds of feet. Stairs were constructed at the backs of the slides for riders to walk up to the top.

Some historians believe the Russians also built the first true roller coaster. This first real coaster was a carriage with wheels that ran along a track. Although there is little evidence, supposedly it was built in St. Petersburg in the late 1700s.

Other historians, however, believe the French built the first coasters with wheels in the early 1800s. Records indicate that two coasters with wheels that locked onto tracks were operating in France around 1817.

From these basic designs, the great roller coasters of today have evolved. Roller coaster fans can only wonder what thrills the coasters of tomorrow will provide.

3.4 Louis Pasteur (1822–1895) was a great French scientist. One of his many important discoveries was a vaccine for rabies.

Rabies is a terrible infection of the nervous system. It is caused by a virus and can infect all warm-blooded animals. To become infected, a person or animal must be bitten by an animal that already has the disease. Before Pasteur's vaccine, rabies almost always was fatal.

In 1885 Pasteur was working on a vaccine for rabies. One day a mother brought her nine-year-old son to Pasteur's laboratory. The boy had been bitten by a rabid dog, and without the vaccine the boy would surely die. But the vaccine had not been tested yet on humans. Although no one knew if it would work, Pasteur agreed to try his vaccine. The vaccine was successful. The boy survived and stayed healthy.

Since then, Pasteur's vaccine has saved thousands of people from rabies. Today, dogs and cats are immunized to prevent them from getting the disease and infecting people.

3.5 A plan of regular exercise is vital for good health. Regular exercise causes you to breathe more deeply, makes your heart pump more vigorously, and makes your muscles work harder. It makes your body use more calories and helps to keep your body at a healthy weight.

Exercising as little as thirty minutes a day, four or five times per week, can keep your body fit. Regular exercise can also help you think better, sleep better, and feel better. Your entire body benefits from exercise.

You can exercise in various ways. You can walk, jog, or play sports. You can work out in a gym. You can ride your bike, skate, swim, or dance. Any activity that makes your heart beat faster for a sustained length of time is beneficial.

Exercise is necessary for your health. You should design a practical exercise plan that fits in with your daily schedule.

3.6 Despite its name, the whale shark is not related to whales at all. Whales are mammals, and sharks are fish. The whale shark is the largest known fish. It may grow to a length of fifty feet and weigh more than twenty tons. This accounts for the "whale" part of its name.

Whale sharks are found in tropical waters around the world. Most of the time they remain in the open sea, but sometimes they are sighted near the shore. They are usually solitary creatures, but they can also be found in schools of dozens or hundreds of individuals.

Whale sharks are known as filter-feeding fish. When feeding, a whale shark swims with its enormous mouth open. Sea water flows into its mouth and filters through its gills. Small fish, shrimp, and plankton (microscopic plants and animals) are caught.

Unlike many sharks, whale sharks are not a threat to humans. In fact, divers who study them may approach them without fear. Some divers have actually ridden whale sharks. The sharks do not seem to mind.

3.7 Pompeii was a Roman city in ancient Italy, a few miles south of Mt. Vesuvius. Mt. Vesuvius was an active volcano then and remains active today. Pompeii was a wealthy city, busy with commerce and trade.

The day of August 24th in the year A.D. 79 began like any other. People awoke, went to work, and began their chores. In the distance Vesuvius sent lazy swirls of dark smoke into the sky. This was normal and no one was worried.

Without warning the summit of Vesuvius exploded. Great clouds of smoke and ash were sent high into the sky. Soon the light of the sun was blocked, and a terrifying shadow descended over the land.

The eruption continued throughout the day and night. Ash and molten rock bombarded the city. Choking smoke and gas made it impossible to breathe. People panicked and tried to flee, but the streets became jammed. People could not get away in time.

The destruction of the city was complete, and an estimated two thousand people died. The doomed city of Pompeii disappeared in a day.

3.8 The Oregon Trail was the most important pioneer route to the American Northwest. About two thousand miles long, the Oregon Trail stretched across the plains and through the mountains. Starting in Independence, Missouri, it ended at the Columbia River in Oregon.

The journey by wagon train over the trail was long, difficult, and dangerous. Because most wagon trains traveled only about fifteen miles per day, the trip could take as long as six months.

The pioneers faced many hardships. They had to survive terrible storms, the threat of starvation, and possible attacks by Native Americans. Disease could strike suddenly and kill entire families. Sometimes as many as half or more of the people of a wagon train died before reaching Oregon.

Despite the hardships and the heartache, thousands of pioneers traveled the trail. They believed that the Oregon Trail would lead them to a new life.

3.9 Joanne Kathleen Rowling was born on July 31, 1965, near Bristol, England. She is known throughout the world as the author of the Harry Potter books.

Rowling thought of the idea of writing a fantasy about Harry Potter, a young wizard, while she was riding a train in 1990. She worked on the first book of the series for the next several years.

When she finished the book, Rowling sent it to publishers. Several turned the book down. Eventually, in 1998, *Harry Potter and the Sorcerer's Stone* was published in the United States. The fantasy focuses on Harry Potter, a lonely orphan who learns that he is a wizard. When Harry enrolls in Hogwarts School of Witchcraft and Wizardry, the magical adventure begins.

The Harry Potter books have proven to be immensely popular. Hundreds of millions of the books have been sold. The books have been translated into more than sixty languages and can be bought in two hundred countries. Movie versions of the books have been equally popular. The magic of Harry Potter continues to enchant fans around the world.

3.10 Vanessa stood in her new room in her family's new house. Boxes were everywhere. In some places they were piled on top of each other right up to the ceiling.

Vanessa sighed. The room was enormous, much bigger than her room in the old house. But the new room did not feel like home. She missed her old house and her old friends. She was worried about making new friends.

After she unpacked a few boxes, Vanessa walked downstairs and went outside. She sat on the front steps. She looked around the big yard at a beautiful rose garden, colorful flower beds, and tall trees. Vanessa had to admit that the yard was pretty, but she doubted she would ever feel at home here.

A little while later, Vanessa noticed a girl at the house across the street. The girl, who was about her own age, started walking toward her.

"Hi, I'm Rebecca," the girl said with a friendly smile. "But my friends call me Becky. . . ."

3.11 Marcus stood in his room. He could not find his history report. He looked around the room and thought of how messy it was. No, he decided. It was more than messy. It was a disaster.

He tried to remember where he had put the report. He had finished it yesterday after school. Then he had played games online with his friends.

He looked at his desk. So many books and papers were piled on it that he could hardly see the top. He searched through each book and piece of paper. Next he searched the stuffed drawers, then he searched through the pants and shirts that lay on his dresser. He even searched under his bed, but all he found there were old sneakers.

Where was the report? He was desperate. Suddenly he remembered.

He picked up his knapsack. He had put the report in the knapsack yesterday so that he would not lose it. He looked inside, and there it was.

Hearing the horn of the school bus, Marcus rushed to the door. He saw the school bus driving away.

3.12 Gabriela stood in front of the big roller coaster. Anthony, her younger brother, stood beside her.

The roller coaster was called the Rocket. It was the biggest and fastest coaster Gabriela had ever seen. She had been looking forward to riding it for weeks, but now she was not sure she wanted to. Gabriela liked fast rides, but this one scared her.

"Come on, Gabriela," said Anthony. "Let's get in line." He took her hand and started pulling her toward the line of people waiting to ride the Rocket.

At first Gabriela did not move. It was as if her feet would not go. She looked at the coaster as it climbed slowly to the top of the tracks. Reaching the peak, it roared down so fast that Gabriela was certain she felt the ground shake.

"Gabriela, come on," said Anthony. "You're not afraid, are you?"

Gabriela smiled. If her little brother was not afraid, she should not be afraid either. She took a deep breath.

"Let's go," Gabriela said. She led Anthony to the line.

3.13 Ten seconds were left in the championship soccer game between the Lions and the Falcons. The score was tied 2 to 2.

Kara Johnson, the Lions' youngest player, was dribbling the ball upfield toward the Falcons' goal. Her heart was pounding, and she was tense. Kara was only in the game because Sharon Wilson, the Lions' best scorer, had been hurt earlier.

As Kara faked out a Falcon defender, she saw a small opening toward the right side of the field. She tried to keep all of her attention focused on the ball. She knew she would have only one chance for a shot.

She dodged another defender and kept moving.

"Take the shot, Kara!" she heard Sharon's voice from the sideline above the noise of the crowd.

Kara looked at the goal. The goalie was in position, staring at her. She knew she could not shoot the ball past her like this.

Kara faked a shot. She took two steps to her left to gain a better angle and kicked the ball as hard as she could.

The goalie could not stop the ball, and Kara watched the ball streak into the goal.

3.14 On a clear night, away from the lights of cities and towns, a person can see a few thousand stars. This is only a tiny part of a universe that contains billions of galaxies. Each galaxy contains billions of stars.

Stars are giant balls of burning gases made up mostly of hydrogen. Inside a star enormous pressure results in nuclear fusion. During fusion, hydrogen atoms are fused, or forced together, to make helium. Great amounts of energy are produced. It is through fusion that the heat and light of a star are created.

In recent years, astronomers have discovered that numerous stars have planets orbiting them. Our solar system no longer appears to be unique. In fact, it may be quite ordinary.

Although we do not yet have the technological capability to travel to distant stars, maybe someday we will. How wondrous it will be to find Earth-like planets in orbit around other stars. Future generations of human beings will make their homes throughout the stars.

3.15 Bears are large mammals. They have heavy bodies, short tails, and rounded ears. Although they are classified as carnivores, or meat-eaters, most bears also eat grasses, herbs, berries, nuts, and honey.

There are several kinds of bears. North American black bears, grizzly bears, and polar bears are among the most well known. North American black bears are native to North America. Black bears are one of the smallest bears and weigh between two hundred and four hundred pounds. Grizzly bears are much larger than black bears and can weigh up to a thousand pounds. Grizzlies may be brown, black, or cream-colored. The fur on their shoulders and backs is often tipped with white, giving them a "grizzled" look. Polar bears are some of the biggest bears. They may be ten feet tall and weigh up to fifteen hundred pounds. They live on the islands of the Arctic Ocean, where they hunt seals, young walruses, and fish.

In the past, bears were found throughout much of the world. Today they are found mostly in wilderness areas.

3.16 On December 16, 1811, a powerful earthquake awakened the residents of New Madrid, Missouri. This was the first of three great earthquakes and thousands of lesser aftershocks that struck the region during the winter of 1811–1812.

Many scientists are convinced that the New Madrid earthquakes were among the most powerful ever experienced in North America. The quakes were so strong that tremors were felt from Canada to Mexico and from the Rocky Mountains to the East Coast. Several towns in the region were destroyed, islands in the Mississippi River disappeared, and new lakes were formed. Eyewitness accounts of survivors reported wide cracks opening in the ground, the ground rolling in waves, and large sections of land rising and sinking. Damage from the quakes was reported as far away as Charleston, South Carolina, and Washington, DC. If such quakes occurred today in the region, the destruction would be unimaginable.

Scientists cannot predict when the next great earthquake will strike the region. Many worry that another major quake is only a matter of time.

3.17 Daniel Hale Williams (1858–1931) was an African-American physician. He performed the first successful heart surgery in 1893.

On July 9th of that year, James Cornish, a young man, was stabbed in the chest. He was brought to Provident Hospital, where Williams was a surgeon. Cornish had lost much blood, and he needed surgery to stop the bleeding. In those days internal operations almost always resulted in death from infection, but Williams knew that without surgery Cornish would die. Williams decided to operate.

During surgery, Williams found that Cornish's pericardium had been wounded. The pericardium is a sac of tissue that surrounds the heart. Williams washed the wound with a salt solution, hoping this would reduce the chance for infection. After stitching the wound, he completed the operation. James Cornish survived and lived for many more years.

Williams went on to become one of the most respected surgeons of his day. In 1913, he became the first African-American to be inducted into the American College of Surgeons.

3.18 With nervous fingers Caitlyn laced her ice skates. She took a deep breath, hoping to steady the uneasiness in her stomach.

"Don't worry," her coach said. "This time you'll do it."

That only made Caitlyn worry more. Caitlyn recalled her first attempt at completing an axel, a jump with one and a half turns in the air. She had jumped, but had fallen on her landing. Caitlyn would forever remember the sharp, knifing pain of her breaking ankle. Months passed before her ankle was fully healed.

Caitlyn had started skating again only a few weeks ago. She had not attempted an axel, but she would today.

Caitlyn stood, stepped onto the ice, and began skating. Her heart was thumping. "You can do it," her coach said.

Caitlyn nodded and forced a weak smile.

She skated around the rink, trying to build up her courage.

Gaining speed, she knew it was now or never. She pushed off the ice, propelled herself into the air, and spun.

Her landing was perfect.

3.19 Arctic terns are small seabirds, but they are champion travelers. They make the longest migration of any bird.

Each year Arctic terns fly from the Arctic to Antarctica, only to return to the Arctic. The total distance is nearly twenty-two thousand miles, approximately the circumference of the Earth.

The terns spend the northern summers in the Arctic tundra, where they breed and make their nests. As the northern winter approaches, the terns begin flying southward until they reach the edge of the Antarctic ice pack. Because the seasons of the northern and southern hemispheres are reversed, it is now summer in Antarctica. Once summer in Antarctica ends, the terns begin flying northward again and return to the Arctic.

Arctic terns are well adapted for their long journeys. They are only twelve to fifteen inches long and weigh less than a pound. They have strong wings and streamlined bodies. They eat small fish, shrimp, and krill, which they catch by swooping down into the water.

Arctic terns have a life span of about twenty years. They spend much of their lives flying.

3.20 The ancient Olympic Games were played in Greece in the wooded valley of Olympia. Beginning in 776 B.C. and continuing until A.D. 393, they were held every four years.

No one knows who organized the first games. According to myth, Hercules, a legendary hero known throughout Greece, started the games. But the poet Pindar, in a poem he wrote in the fifth century B.C., claimed a warrior named Pelops created the games to celebrate a great victory.

The first Olympics were rather small. Only one event was held. This was the stade, a footrace of about two hundred yards. In time, a forty-thousand-seat stadium was built, and more races, wrestling, chariot racing, and the pentathlon were added. The pentathlon was a five-part event that included running, wrestling, jumping, and throwing the discus and javelin.

The Olympics were enormously popular. People from all over Greece came to watch the games. In times of war, truces were called to allow athletes and spectators to travel to Olympia safely. It is upon this grand tradition that the modern Olympic Games are founded.

3.21 When you see a bird, you are looking at a descendant of a dinosaur. Many scientists are now convinced that birds are directly related to the dinosaurs that walked the Earth millions of years ago.

The evidence for the dinosaur–bird link is strong. Just like modern birds, many dinosaurs walked on their hind legs, they had three forward-pointing toes, and they had long tails. In the 1990s, paleontologists found fossils of dinosaurs in northeastern China that had evidence of feathers. Soon more fossilized skeletons of dinosaurs were found that showed evidence of feathers and other birdlike features.

The best evidence came in 2000. Paleontologists found the fossil of a small dinosaur that they named *Microraptor zhaoianus*. It was about the size of a crow and closely resembled a bird.

Despite the evidence of birdlike features, most scientists do not consider these dinosaurs to be true birds. It is more likely these creatures are a link between dinosaurs and birds.

The dinosaurs are extinct, but their descendants are alive and well.

3.22 The Maya were among the most advanced native civilizations of the Americas. Starting around 2600 B.C., the Maya slowly gained power and influence. They came to control much of the land that is now southern Mexico, Guatemala, Belize, and Honduras.

From about A.D. 200 through 900, their society was among the most advanced in the world. The Maya constructed great cities, magnificent buildings, and pyramids that served as temples. They developed hieroglyphic writing and an accurate calendar. Mayan astronomers recorded the movements of the sun, planets, and stars.

Around 900, the Maya started to decline. No one knows why. Some historians believe wars, disease, and crop failures over a period of years might have caused the decline. This much is known. Cities in southern areas were abandoned, and the cities of the north were overcome by an invading group known as the Toltecs.

When the Spanish arrived in the sixteenth century, only a few Mayan cities remained. The great civilization was gone.

3.23 On Saturday morning Darien woke up much earlier than he usually did. He had much to do.

After a quick breakfast of cereal, milk, and juice, Darien rode his bike to soccer practice. He was the goalie for his team. He liked soccer and had been playing soccer since first grade.

After lunch, Darien helped his father with work around the house. They planted five new shrubs on the side of the house. As his father watered the shrubs, Darien weeded the flower beds. After they finished the yard work, they cleaned the garage for the rest of the afternoon.

After dinner, Darien's friends, Peter and Ricky, came over. The boys decided to play video games. They played several games, and the evening passed quickly.

By the time his friends went home, Darien was exhausted. As he went to bed, Darien thought of all the things he had to do tomorrow.

222

Answer Key

3.24 Kangaroos are found in Australia and on nearby islands. Most people are not aware that there are about a hundred different species, or kinds, of kangaroos. They range from the tiny kangaroo rat to the giant kangaroo.

The giant kangaroo, also called the great gray kangaroo, is one of the best-known species of kangaroo. Giant kangaroos stand about five feet tall and weigh up to 150 pounds. They have sheeplike heads, big ears, short front legs, long tails, and large, powerful hind legs. With its powerful legs, a giant kangaroo can jump thirty feet in a single hop and reach speeds of up to forty miles per hour.

Kangaroos are marsupials. Like other female marsupials, female kangaroos carry their young in pouches. A female kangaroo carries her young one, called a joey, in her pouch until it is old enough to survive on its own.

Kangaroos are timid creatures, but when attacked, they can be dangerous. They will use their forepaws to "punch" an attacker. They will also use their hind legs to kick and slash. A large kangaroo can seriously injure a person.

3.25 In ancient Greek mythology, Phaeton was the son of Apollo, the god of the sun. One day Phaeton went to his father's magnificent palace of the sun. Apollo was so pleased to see his son that he promised to grant Phaeton anything he asked.

Phaeton had one desire. He wanted to drive Apollo's chariot of the sun across the sky.

Apollo knew this could not be. He warned his son that no one else—not even the other gods—could drive the chariot of the sun.

Phaeton would not be swayed from his demand, and Apollo reluctantly agreed.

Phaeton climbed into the chariot and whipped the horses. The mighty animals galloped into the sky, pulling the bright sun behind the chariot. But Phaeton quickly lost control of them. They ran low to the Earth, and the blazing sun burned the ground and all on it.

When Zeus, king of the gods, realized Earth was being destroyed, he hurled a lightning bolt at Phaeton. The boy was killed, and the Earth was saved.

From that day on, all understood that only Apollo could drive the sun's chariot across the sky. They knew that a person should not try to seize control of natural forces.

Part 4

In a few articles and stories, corrections may vary depending on context. This is particularly true in the case of commas. Corrected articles and stories follow.

4.1 If you have ever been caught in a thunderstorm, you may have been frightened by the lightning and thunder. Have you ever wondered what causes lightning and thunder?

The air within a thunderstorm is turbulent. As warm air rises and cool air falls, water droplets and ice crystals crash into each other. These collisions cause electrical charges to build up. Positive charges collect in the upper parts of the clouds, and negative charges collect in the lower parts. To balance the negative charges, positive charges also collect near the ground. As this process continues, the charges increase in strength. Because unlike charges attract, electricity may jump from one cloud to another or between a cloud and the ground. We see this as lightning.

A lightning bolt is extremely hot. It heats air molecules and causes them to expand violently. This causes a powerful vibration that we hear as thunder.

Thunder can be loud and frightening, but lightning is dangerous. When a thunderstorm approaches, you should seek shelter indoors. Stay away from windows and doors, and do not use electrical equipment. If you are outside, never stand near a tree. Trees can attract lightning. A lightning strike can be fatal.

4.2 Many students do not know how to study for tests. Are you one of them? If you think you are, the following tips can help.

Preparation for any test begins long before the day of the test. Keep up with your daily work and take accurate notes. On the days leading up to the test, listen to any reviews your teacher gives. This will help you to identify what may be on the test. This in turn will help you to study the right material. If you have any questions about any of the material, ask your teacher.

A day or two before the test, you should go over your notes and key parts of your textbook. Do not wait until the last minute to study. Students who study ahead of time usually do better than those who cram at the last minute.

Get a good night's sleep before the test, wake up on time, and eat a solid breakfast. Take the test with confidence. If you have studied effectively, you are likely to do well.

4.3 Martina woke up early on Thanksgiving morning. Anxious to start the day, she dressed quickly and scampered downstairs.

She found her mother in the kitchen preparing food to take to Martina's grandmother's house. That was where the entire family gathered every Thanksgiving for dinner. All of Martina's uncles, aunts, and cousins would be there.

After breakfast, Martina helped her mother pack food in a big cooler. They packed salad, fresh vegetables, fruits, and two cream pies.

Martina's grandmother lived about three hours away, and the drive seemed to take forever. As they drove, Martina wondered how many family members had already arrived. When Martina's father pulled into the driveway, she saw several cars.

Martina smiled. Everyone was here. Having Thanksgiving with the family was always a wonderful time.

4.4 Frogs are interesting creatures. They go through metamorphosis, a complete change in structure during their lives. They begin life as a fishlike tadpole and grow into a frog.

Tadpoles hatch from eggs. They breathe with gills, have streamlined bodies, and have tails. They feed on algae and tiny vegetation.

As a tadpole matures, its gills disappear, lungs develop, and legs start to grow. In time the tadpole starts eating insects and larger plant matter.

After about nine weeks of life, the tadpole looks more like a frog with a tail than a tadpole. Eventually the tail is absorbed into the tadpole's body. By about the fourth month of its life, a tadpole has made the transition to a frog. Metamorphosis is finished.

The cycle is now ready to repeat. Female frogs lay their eggs in water, from which a new generation of tadpoles hatches.

4.5 Madam C. J. Walker (1867–1919) was the most successful African-American businesswoman of the early twentieth century. She became the first African-American woman millionaire.

Madam Walker, whose birth name was Sarah Breedlove, built a company that sold hair products for African-American women. To help the company grow, Madam Walker tirelessly promoted her products. By 1910, her company had become so successful that she was able to put others in charge of the day-to-day operations. This allowed her to devote more time to lecture on issues that affected African-Americans. In her later years, Madam Walker supported numerous African-American schools, charities, and organizations.

When Madam Walker died at the age of fifty-one, she was thought to be the wealthiest African-American woman in the United States. Her life was an inspiration to women throughout the country.

4.6 Samantha hurried down the empty hallway toward her classroom. School had ended an hour ago, and she hoped her classroom was not locked. She needed to get her science book, which she had forgotten to take home. Without the book, she wouldn't be able to study for the big science test tomorrow.

Science was a difficult subject for Samantha. She had to study more for science than for any other subject.

When she got to her classroom, Samantha was relieved to find the door open. She went inside, expecting to see Mrs. Talbot, her teacher, but the room was empty. Samantha figured that Mrs. Talbot had gone home for the day.

As Samantha walked by the teacher's desk, she noticed a paper on it. Her eyes widened. It was the answer key to the test. The key could help her get a good grade.

Samantha stood there for a long moment. Taking the answers would be cheating, and that was wrong.

She went to her desk, got her science book, and left the room.

4.7 People have dreamed about flying for thousands of years. Early ideas ranged from mechanical wings that could enable a person to fly like a bird to strange machines with flapping blades. None, of course, worked.

As time passed, people looked for other ways to fly. A breakthrough came in France in 1782.

Joseph and Jacques Montgolfier, two brothers, were interested in flying. While sitting by a fireplace, Joseph filled a paper bag with smoke and hot air. As the brothers watched the bag float up to the ceiling, they got an idea.

The Montgolfiers began to experiment. They made balloons out of paper and linen and filled them with hot air from a fire. When they released the balloons, the balloons rose. The brothers built bigger and bigger balloons until they built one able to carry people.

Finally, in November of 1783, two people flew in a Montgolfier balloon. This first flight lasted twenty-five minutes and covered about five miles. The dream of flight became a reality.

4.8 Earthquakes may best be described as a shaking of the Earth. Thousands of earthquakes occur each year, but only one out of five is strong enough to be felt. On average, of every thousand earthquakes only two cause damage.

Earthquakes are caused by movement of the Earth's crust. The Earth's crust, which is its outer layer, is divided into great pieces. These pieces, called plates, are made of rock. The plates move slowly in different directions. They may grind past each other, away from each other, or toward each other. Sometimes a long crack, called a fault, forms between plates. The famous San Andreas Fault in California is a result of two plates grinding past each other. If enough stress builds up along a fault, an earthquake occurs.

Minor earthquakes cause little damage and few injuries. Major quakes can destroy entire cities and result in thousands of deaths.

4.9 It was the biggest regional track meet of the season. Andrew stretched and tried to shake the nervous tension from his body. So far this year he had won all of the two-mile races he had entered, but now he was facing boys who might be faster and have greater endurance.

The official called the boys to the starting line. Andrew took a deep breath and stepped forward.

"Remember, Andrew," Coach Simmons said, "pace yourself. Make sure you're strong for the end."

Andrew nodded. He took his position on the inside lane. He thought about his coach's advice. Andrew sometimes made the mistake of running too hard in the first part of a race. When he did that, he would fade at the end.

"On your mark!" said the official. "Get set! Go!"

The race began.

Andrew was in the middle of the pack of runners, his strides long and easy. It was a long way to the end of the race. He would make sure he was strong for the finish.

4.10

123 River Drive
Green Valley, NJ 00000
Oct. 25, 2010

Ms. Janice Williams, Circulation Manager
Extreme Skateboarding Magazine
50 Reynolds Street
Mountain Lake, CA 00000

Dear Ms. Williams:

I would like to subscribe to *Extreme Skateboarding Magazine*. Enclosed is a check for $24.95 for a subscription for one year.
Thank you.

Sincerely yours,
Thomas Jackson

4.11 Richie and I are best friends. We've been best friends for about as long as I can remember.

Some kids think it's strange that a girl and boy in seventh grade are best friends. But I don't think it's strange at all. Richie and I have a lot in common.

We've always lived next door to each other. We both like sports, we like the same type of music, and we like the same kinds of movies. But most important, we just like hanging out together. There's never any trouble between Richie and me. We stick up for each other, and we're always honest with each other. Richie's easy to talk to, and he's always willing to help when I have a problem. I do the same for him.

No matter what happens, I know I can depend on Richie, and he knows he can depend on me. I suppose that, most of all, is what makes our friendship so special.

4.12 What happened to Amelia Earhart? People have been trying to answer this question since 1937. That was the year Earhart and Fred J. Noonan, her copilot, disappeared in their plane near Howland Island in the South Pacific.

Amelia Earhart loved to fly. She became famous in May of 1932 when she made a solo flight across the Atlantic Ocean. She followed this feat with several solo long-distance flights across the U.S. In January of 1931, she made a solo flight from Hawaii to California.

Earhart attempted her most daring flight in June of 1937. With copilot Noonan, she set off to make an around-the-world flight. On July 2nd their plane vanished. Rescue teams mounted extensive search efforts, but no sign of Earhart, Noonan, or their plane was ever found.

In the following years, researchers and mystery buffs have tried to discover what happened to Amelia Earhart. None have succeeded, and Amelia Earhart's disappearance remains a mystery.

4.13 Giorgio stared at the overcast sky. He turned to Danny, his friend.

"It looks like rain," Giorgio said.

"According to the weather forecast," said Danny, "there's only a slight chance of showers."

The two boys had just arrived at the baseball field for the first game of the season. Some of the players of both teams were already there.

Coach Bennett instructed the boys to begin warming up.

Giorgio and Danny took their places with their teammates and began playing catch.

Giorgio looked back at the sky. Baseball was his favorite sport, and he had been looking forward to this first game for weeks.

"Giorgio, quit worrying," said Danny. "The game will start on time."

"I hope so," said Giorgio.

A little while later, the sun poked through the clouds.

"See," said Danny. "The sun's coming out. Now you'll be worrying about the sun getting into your eyes."

Giorgio smiled. "You're probably right."

4.14 Step into my house, and you will find books and magazines everywhere. Everybody in my family enjoys reading. We read for entertainment and information.

My father rides the bus to work each morning. During his commute he reads *The New York Times*. He also reads magazines. His favorites are *Time* and *Discover*.

My mother enjoys reading novels. She reads a new novel every week. She likes mysteries the best, but she also likes romances. Sometimes she likes a book so much that she can't put it down until she finishes it.

Jessica, my older sister, likes short stories and poems. One of her favorite short stories is "The Dinner Party" by Mona Gardner. Her favorite poem is Lewis Carroll's "Jabberwocky."

As for me, I mostly read novels. My favorites are fantasies with heroes, evil villains, and magic. If I had to pick one favorite, I would choose *The Hobbit* by J. R. R. Tolkien.

4.15 Emily stuck her ski poles into the snow to steady herself. She stood on the top of the mountain and looked down the slope. Daredevil Trail disappeared in the distance.

She felt a gentle pat on her shoulder.

"You can make it down," said Alyssa, her big sister.

"That's not what worries me," said Emily. She forced a smile. "I'm worried about how many broken bones I'll have."

"You don't have to do this," Alyssa said.

"Yes, I do," said Emily, who prided herself on her skill at skiing. "This is the only trail on this mountain I've never gone down."

Alyssa smiled. "You'll be fine," she said. "Keep your knees bent and remember to lean into the turns."

Emily nodded. "Here I go." She pushed off with her poles and started down the trail.

She heard Alyssa's voice behind her.

"You can do it."

As Emily leaned into the first turn, she hoped her sister was right.

4.16 The sounds of laughter, the honking of a car horn, and the roar of a lawn mower's motor are all produced in the same way. But do you know how those sounds are produced?

All sounds are a result of vibrations. When something vibrates, it moves back and forth rapidly. Imagine plucking a string on a violin. As the string vibrates, it makes a sound. Of course, you seldom see the vibrations that cause sound, because the vibrations are too small and are moving too fast. Unlike plucking a string, imagine tapping a pencil on a desk. You can't see the vibrations, but you hear the sound of the tapping.

When an object vibrates, it causes the nearby molecules in the air to move. As the molecules move, the vibrations travel through the air in the form of waves. Like the ripples that result from a stone tossed in a pond, the waves move outward from the point of the sound in every direction. When these waves reach your ear, you hear the sound.

As sound waves move outward from a vibrating object, they become weaker. This is why a sound becomes fainter the farther away you are from its source.

4.17 Have you ever played chess? If you have, you have played a game that has been around for at least fifteen hundred years.

Chess is a game of skill and strategy played by two players. The game is based on the warfare of the Middle Ages. Each player has sixteen pieces that he plays on a square board. The board is divided into sixty-four alternate light and dark squares. When a player lands a piece on a space occupied by one of his opponent's pieces, that piece is removed from the board. The object of the game is to capture, or checkmate, the opponent's king. Capture of the king ends the game.

No one knows who invented chess. Most historians believe the game originated in India about the sixth century A.D. The game slowly spread westward through Persia (modern Iran) and reached Europe sometime between 700 and 900.

The modern game began to evolve during the sixteenth and seventeenth centuries. Today, chess is played around the world and is as popular as ever.

4.18 A volcano is a mountain with a vent, or opening, to the interior of the Earth. Magma (hot, melted rock) from inside the Earth passes through the vent to the surface. Sometimes the magma flows out slowly, but sometimes it erupts in great explosions.

Volcanoes can be in one of three states: active, dormant, or extinct. An active volcano is erupting or shows signs of erupting soon. A dormant volcano has not erupted in some time but may erupt again in the future. An extinct volcano is no longer capable of erupting.

Volcanic eruptions start far beneath the surface. When magma comes under great pressure, it rises through cracks and weak spots in the rock. Eventually the magma finds its way to the surface. If the pressure is intense, the magma may erupt. Along with magma, eruptions usually include gases, ash, and steam.

Magma that flows out of a volcano is called lava. Lava can reach temperatures of 2,000 degrees Fahrenheit or more. Flowing down a volcano's sides, lava can destroy everything in its path.

Scientists study volcanoes in the hope of learning how to predict eruptions. Such knowledge would help them warn people before an eruption occurs.

4.19 Brianna stepped from the dock and into the boat. She plopped onto the nearest seat. She was not happy being here. She and her parents were about to spend one of their vacation days in search of whales. Brianna would have preferred to spend the day at the oceanside resort where the family was staying for the week.

"I've been looking forward to today for months," Brianna's mother said.

"I haven't," Brianna said. "I'd rather be at the beach."

"You can go to the beach every day for the rest of our vacation," said her father. "But if we're lucky, today you can see a whale."

Brianna didn't like boats, and she liked the idea of searching for whales even less.

As the boat left the dock, Brianna sighed. This was going to be a long day.

It was early afternoon when the captain directed everyone to look ahead.

"There!" cried one of the passengers.

Brianna looked and saw a magnificent animal rise from the water.

"It's incredible," she said, suddenly glad she was here and not back on the beach.

4.20 One of the most wonderful features of the world is color. Colors help to make things distinct. Just think of a blue sky, a red rose, or the pure whiteness of freshly fallen snow. Can you imagine how dull the world would be without color?

The basics of colors are surprisingly simple. Colors can be divided into three kinds: primary, secondary, and intermediate. The primary colors are red, yellow, and blue. They can't be made by mixing any other colors. The secondary colors, which are made by mixing two primary colors, are orange, green, and violet. Mixing red and yellow makes orange. Mixing yellow and blue makes green. Mixing blue and red makes violet. Intermediate colors are made by mixing primary and secondary colors. Mixing white or black with colors will make them lighter or darker.

It's remarkable that all colors are based on combinations of red, yellow, and blue. The world truly is a colorful place.

4.21 I was upstairs working on my book report when Marlena, my little sister, called me from downstairs.

"Come quick, Angela!" she cried.

"What's wrong?" I said, getting up from my desk and hurrying to the stairs.

"It's Puffin!" Marlena said. "She's in a big tree. She can't get down." Puffin was our cat.

I hurried downstairs and followed Marlena out the front door.

Looking up at the big oak tree in our yard, I saw Puffin sitting on a high branch. She had climbed up, but she was afraid to climb down.

"Puffin, come down right now," I said. A mournful meow was my answer.

There wasn't anything I could do except to keep calling Puffin down. But the cat wouldn't budge.

I was glad when my father came home from work. He got a ladder, climbed up, and got Puffin.

I smiled as Marlena scolded the foolish cat.

"Puffin, I never want you to climb that tree again," she said.

4.22 If you have ever seen a rainbow in the sky, you have witnessed one of the beauties of nature. The typical rainbow makes an arc in the sky. Sometimes a rainbow is so big that its ends seem to touch the Earth.

The mystery of a rainbow lies in sunlight and water droplets. A ray of sunlight contains all the colors of the spectrum: red, orange, yellow, green, blue, and violet. When sunlight shines through water droplets, the droplets separate the sunlight into its different colors. Under the right conditions this creates a rainbow.

Rainbows may appear anywhere sunlight shines on water droplets, but they most often are seen near the end of a rain shower. They may also appear in the spray of a waterfall, a fountain, or a garden hose.

According to legend, a pot of gold awaits you at the end of a rainbow. Of course, you can never reach the end. As you approach a rainbow, the rainbow seems to retreat and soon disappears.

4.23 Dawn walked up the steps to the home of Mr. and Mrs. Ross and rang the doorbell. This was the first time she was to babysit for Matthew, their son. She hoped Matthew, who was only five years old, would behave. Christina, Dawn's best friend, babysat for Matthew once, and she vowed never to babysit for him again.

Mrs. Ross opened the door and greeted Dawn with a friendly smile.

Dawn saw Matthew standing in the living room. He was smiling too. He seemed like a nice boy.

After Mrs. Ross gave Dawn instructions, she and her husband got ready to leave.

"Remember, Dawn," Mrs. Ross said at the door, "Matthew must be in bed no later than nine o'clock."

"I'll remember," Dawn said.

For the next two hours Dawn read to Matthew, they drew and colored, and they watched Matthew's favorite video. Matthew was so pleasant that Dawn began to wonder if Christina had babysat for the same boy.

At nine o'clock Dawn told Matthew that it was time for bed.

Matthew looked at her and smiled.

"No!" he said firmly. "And you can't make me go to bed."

Dawn thought of Christina and realized that it was going to be a long night.

4.24 It was the final day of wrestling camp. Dan was to wrestle Brett in the championship match for their weight class.

Dan looked at Brett and frowned. He doubted that he could defeat Brett. Brett was a year older and had more experience.

"Brett's a great wrestler," Dan said to Roberto, his best friend.

"He is," said Roberto, "but he loses his cool. He likes to pin his opponents fast. But when that doesn't happen, he gets mad and makes mistakes."

"But how does that help me?" said Dan. "He's faster and stronger than I am."

"You have to wrestle smart," said Roberto. "Don't let him gain the advantage. He'll get frustrated and then you make your move."

"You mean stay on defense until he makes a mistake," said Dan.

Roberto nodded.

Soon after the match began, Dan realized his friend was right. When the match was finished, Dan was a wrestling champion.

4.25 Commander Sarto stood on the bridge of his starship and watched the main viewing screen. As they approached the tiny planet, it grew on the screen. Sarto studied the oceans and land masses that appeared through the clouds. The planet reminded him of home.

"Take us into orbit," he said to Jartan, his second in command. "Then see if you can listen to their communications."

Sarto thought of his mission to make contact with the beings that lived on the planet. He wondered what they were like.

He noticed the concern that had come to Jartan's face.

"What's the matter?" Sarto said.

"There must be some mistake," said Jartan. "The transmissions I'm picking up indicate that these beings are quite violent. They're not ready to join the United Planets."

Sarto sighed. He had seen this happen before.

"Sometimes the first survey teams make errors in their evaluations," Sarto said. "Set course for the next planet. Make a note to visit Earth again in about a hundred years."